EVERYDAY BENTO

50 Cute and Yummy Lunches To Go

Wendy Thorpe Copley

TUTTLE Publishing

Tokyo | Rutland, Vermont | Singapore

Contents

Introduction

"Bento" is the Japanese word for meals that are packed into boxes and eaten on the go. If you were to expand that definition a little, they are also well-balanced with a blend of flavors, textures, and colors.

Although bento meals have long been a staple of Japanese culture, they are a fairly recent export to the United States. The last few years has seen an increase in the popularity of bento lunches here in America for a variety of reasons. The cheerful presentations and variety of healthy foods incorporated into bentos appeal to parents attempting to entice picky kids to eat a balanced diet, while adults are drawn to this style of lunches for themselves because they are economically and environmentally friendly.

Many people like the idea of packing bento lunches, but they assume they're complex and time consuming to put together. In actuality, packing an attractive bento box doesn't require a lot of time or specialized skills. Armed with the right tools and some basic techniques anyone can make beautiful bento meals that are a delicious everyday treat.

Traditional bento box lunches often feature foods that are popular in Japan. The ingredients for these dishes can be difficult to find and sometimes they're so rare in the States that many people have never even heard of them. While the lunches in this book use some Japanese packing techniques, they are based around ingredients that are common in the American diet and – even more importantly – these ingredients are readily available in large chain grocery stores.

I've filled this book with simple techniques anyone can master to make bento box lunches for themselves and their families. My hope is that in addition to using the detailed instructions provided to recreate the projects presented here, readers will take the techniques they learn while making these lunches and combine them in new ways to make unique meals of their own design. These versatile techniques can be used in endless combinations to make lunch packing – and eating – more creative and fun.

Wendy Thorpe Copley

ROCK 'N' ROLL
THE BENTOS

Bento Box Basics

THE BENEFITS OF MAKING BENTO BOX LUNCHES

THEY'RE FUN! Making decorative bentos is an enjoyable creative outlet. Mornings can be hectic and full of chores, but taking a few minutes to make a beautiful bento box starts the day off on a positive note.

THEY'RE ECONOMICAL. Packing lunches at home to bring to school or work saves money. You don't have to pay for a restaurant lunch and you also save money by reinventing a leftover chicken breast, tucking in the remaining berries from breakfast, or using the last few vegetables in the crisper.

THEY GENERATE LESS WASTE. Fast-food meals and school lunches generate a great deal of packaging waste, and traditional sack lunches with their plastic bags and single serving snacks aren't much better. Packing food into a reusable box with reusable accessories generates no waste at all.

YOU HAVE BETTER CONTROL OVER INGREDIENTS. The only way to know exactly what food you or your child is eating is to make it yourself. With bento boxes you are free to choose organic fruits and vegetables, nitrite-free meats, and foods that are lower in sodium. You can also indulge in the occasional not-so-healthy treat if you like, but the choice is yours.

Basic Techniques

BALANCE
An important goal when making a bento is to balance the types of foods in the box—proteins, produce, grains—and also to achieve a variety of flavors and textures. Shoot for packing at least five different colors into your bentos. This helps to ensure that you're getting lots of healthy fruits and veggies in your bento box.

PACK THE BOX TIGHTLY
When you're packing a bento it is important to fill the box completely. If the food isn't packed snugly and filled up to the top rim of the box, everything will mix together and the little bit of extra time you spent to make your meal attractive will have been wasted. When you pack a bento tightly, there's no extra space in the box and if there aren't any extra spaces, the food will stay in place when the box is tilted because it won't have anywhere to go. After you pack the main components, look for any extra spaces. If you find some, plug them up with smaller bites. Grapes, cubes of cheese, berries, and cherry tomatoes are wonderful for filling these little gaps. If you are using a box with a lot of dividers, this is less of a concern because the dividers will keep things from moving around.

PACK THE BOX NEATLY
One of the easiest ways to make a bento look attractive is simply to pack it neatly. Think about where each item will go before you put it in the box. When items are added, take a few seconds to decide on the best way to present them—crackers can be stacked, vegetable sticks lined up, and any marred pieces of fruit can be tucked under prettier ones.

ENJOY IT!
Most importantly, have fun! Enjoy the beauty of colorful fruit and vegetables and think of creative ways to use your supplies. Add something that will make the person you're packing the lunch for smile, or if you're packing for yourself, put in a favorite treat to make your lunch extra special.

Equipment

BOXES

The most important item to get when you start packing bento lunches is a box. Bento boxes come in all sorts of shapes, materials, configurations, and prices. They range in size from small snack boxes to large thermal systems and they can be purchased for as little as a few dollars for a small plastic box or as much as $70 for a large stainless steel kit. It can be difficult to decide which kind of box to buy and, unfortunately, there's no one-size-fits-all solution to the problem. Some of the factors one should consider when choosing a box are how much food the box needs to hold, the material it's made from, the cost, and how durable it is.

Single-tier Bento Boxes Single-tier boxes are one of the most plentiful types of boxes. They are usually about 1½ inches (4 cm) deep, but their other dimensions vary widely. These boxes usually seal with a tight-fitting hinged lid, but self-sealing lids are also common. If you have a hard time finding a bento box you like, or you're not ready to invest in one yet, food storage containers are often well suited for bento packing.

Multi-tier Bento Boxes Stacking or multi-tier boxes are also quite common. Typically they have at least three parts—a lid and two tiers that hold food. They may also have a third or fourth tier to hold food, an inner lid for each tier, and a tier designed to hold silverware or chopsticks. These boxes often require an additional elastic band or "belt" to hold the tiers closed, though some models are sealed with a hinged lid.

Lunch box systems Many manufacturers sell lunch box systems that are designed to include everything you need to pack a lunch and send it to school, day care, or the office. All of these systems come with some sort of divided container to hold food. Some are a simple divided box with a lid, others have an outer container with several removable inner containers. Systems might also include a thermal lunch bag, an ice pack, and cutlery.

Tools

The list of tools and accessories you can use to make decorative bento box meals is truly endless. Here are just a few examples of the items I used to make the lunches in this book.

Knives and scissors A good, sharp paring knife is the most important tool you'll need to make bento lunches. Use it to slice fruits and vegetables, cube cheese, cut sandwiches into strips or triangles, just as a start. Even if a knife is the only tool you have, you can make a beautiful bento. Kitchen shears or fine-tipped scissors perform many of the same tasks as knives, but they give you an extra level of control. Use them to cut bread or cheese into shapes using a template or for more free-form designs.

Toothpicks and skewers The tips of toothpicks and bamboo skewers can be used to precisely place small elements in a design or reach into places where fingers don't fit. The blunt end of a pick is great for dabbing mayonnaise onto small pieces of food when you're "gluing" a decoration down. Toothpicks can also be used to make kebabs or decorative picks.

Silicone cups Silicone cups are used in most of the bento boxes in this book and for good reason! They can separate dry items from juicy ones, or keep small items like peas or berries from rolling all over the bento box. They are flexible enough to conform to the space available and because they're made from silicone they're almost indestructible. These cups also add a bright spot of color to a lunch and shaped ones can be used to emphasize a theme. Round cups intended for cupcakes are a good shape to start with.

Lidded containers Use small, lidded containers to pack dips and salad dressing. Larger ones can be

Knives and scissors

Toothpicks and skewers

Silicone cups

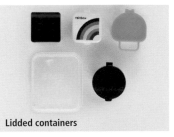

Lidded containers

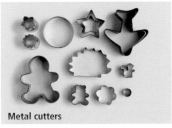

Metal cutters

used for kid-sized portions of yogurt or applesauce.

Metal cutters Metal cutters are an excellent choice for making bento lunches because they're sturdy and they cut through almost any food with ease—bread, fruit, cheese, and even firmer vegetables. They are available in endless shapes and sizes. You can find a cutter to fit almost any theme, but if you are just starting your collection, it's best to stock up with the basics—circles, stars, flowers, and hearts.

Plastic cutters Plastic cutters are nearly as plentiful as metal ones and they tend to be a bit more economical. Purchase them in themed sets or variety packs, or raid your kids' modeling clay sets for basic shapes. If you can find them, Japanese sets with lots of small cutters for making faces are a great option.

Sandwich cutters Larger sandwich cutters are a fast way to add character to a lunch. A quick cut trims the crusts off bread and gives you a decorative shape.

Stamping cutters Plunger or stamping cutters are dual purpose. Use the outside edge to cut basic shapes, then use the detailed insert to stamp an image onto bread or cheese.

Decorative picks Decorative picks are cute *and* functional! Thread with chunks of fruit, veggies, meat, or cheese for an appealing presentation, or use them as mini utensils to eat your food at lunchtime. You can buy sturdy plastic picks designed specifically for bentos, or keep an eye out for paper cupcake picks in kitchen supply stores.

Food dividers Slip decorative food dividers between foods with incompatible flavors or textures in your bento box to keep their flavors from melding. Or add them for a quick spot of color and fun.

Food-safe markers Several baking supply companies make these markers, which use food coloring rather than traditional ink. Use them to draw details on bread, cheese, crackers, and other dry, firm surfaces.

Egg molds Pop a warm hard-boiled egg into one of these molds, let it sit a few minutes, then remove it to find it transformed.

Rice molds Available from retailers that sell Japanese goods, rice molds are used to shape cooked rice into decorative shapes.

Punches Use punches designed specifically for bento lunches to punch faces or other shapes out of nori seaweed. Regular paper punches designed for crafting can also be used for this purpose.

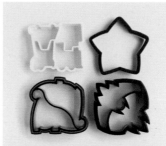

Sandwich cutters

Stamping cutters

Decorative picks

Food dividers

Food-safe markers

Egg molds

Rice molds

Punches

Bento Box Idea List

Often the most difficult part of packing a bento box is figuring out what foods to put in it! Use this list to trigger ideas before you go shopping.

GRAINS

Bagels
Banana bread, zucchini bread, or other quick breads
Cereal bars
Cheese crackers
Dinner rolls
Dry cereal
Flatbread
French bread
Granola bars
Mini-muffins
Pancakes
Pasta
Pita bread
Pretzels
Rice
Rice cakes
Tortillas
Waffles
Whole grain crackers

FRUITS

Apple
Applesauce
Banana
Berries
Canned fruit, drained and rinsed
Cherries
Dried fruit—raisins, dried cranberries, etc.
Figs
Grapefruit
Grapes
Kiwi
Mango
Melon
Nectarine
Orange or clementine
Peach
Pineapple

VEGGIES

Artichoke
Avocado
Bell pepper
Broccoli
Carrot
Cauliflower
Celery
Corn
Cucumber
Edamame
Green beans
Lettuce
Olives
Peas
Radish
Sugar snap peas
Tomatoes

PROTEINS

Baked tofu
Beans
Bean dip
Beef
Chicken
Ham
Hard-boiled eggs
Meatballs
Pastrami
Peanut butter
Salami
Sausages
Turkey
Smoked salmon or other fish

DAIRY

Cheese cubes
Cheese slices
Cottage cheese
Cream cheese
Individual cheeses: string cheese, Babybel, etc.
Yogurt

Bento Foods by Color

When you are creating a themed lunch, food acts as a sort of paintbox you use to create an image or a mood. Use this chart as a guide when you are stumped!

WHITE
Cheese
Chicken
Couscous
Cream cheese
Egg
Grits
Pasta
Peeled apple
Popcorn
Pork
Potatoes
Rice
Tofu
Turkey
White bread

BROWN
Bacon
Bagel
Beef
Cereal
Chocolate
Crackers
Hamburger
Lamb
Meatballs
Nuts
Pinto beans
Pretzels
Sausage
Whole-wheat bread

BLACK
Black beans
Black grapes
Black olives
Blackberries
Raisins

PINK
Ham
Hot dog
Salmon
Shrimp
Watermelon

RED
Cherries
Dried cranberries
Raspberries
Red apple
Red pepper
Red tomatoes
Salami
Strawberries
Watermelon

ORANGE
Apricot
Cantaloupe
Carrot
Cheddar cheese
Dried apricots
Mango
Orange pepper
Orange
Peach

YELLOW
Applesauce
Banana
Corn
Pineapple
Yellow pepper
Yellow tomatoes

GREEN
Artichoke
Asparagus
Avocado
Broccoli
Brussels sprouts
Celery
Cucumber
Edamame
Green apple
Green beans
Green grapes
Green olives
Green pepper
Lettuce
Peas
Pickles
Sugar snap peas
Zucchini

BLUE
Blueberries

PURPLE
Plums
Red grapes

BENTOS
FOR BUSY
MORNINGS

Bear Cub Bento

A little bear sandwich is nestled in a bear-shaped box along with his favorite food — berries, acorns, and fish he just scooped from the river!

INGREDIENTS
Sliced whole-wheat bread
Desired sandwich fillings
Blackberries
Blueberries
Fish-shaped crackers
1 Babybel cheese

EQUIPMENT
Two-tier bear-shaped bento box
Large bear cutter
Fine-tipped kitchen scissors
Round silicone baking cup (I used a blue
    cup to represent water)
Small acorn cutter

❶ Cut bear shapes from the bread. Assemble the sandwich using your desired sandwich fillings. Place the sandwich in one tier of the box.

❷ Use scissors to carefully cut two juice pods from one of the blackberries (the technical name for these is drupelets). Place on the bread to give the bear eyes.

❸ Fill the empty space around the bear with the blueberries.

❹ Put the fish-shaped crackers in the silicone cup and place in the second tier of the bento box.

❺ Place the acorn cheese (see facing page) in the box. Fill the remaining space with the blackberries.

Variations *Small circles of fruit leather or dabs of jelly could also be used for the bear's eyes.*

DECORATING A CHEESE WITH A CUTOUT

1. To cut a shape from the wax around a small cheese (Babybel brand, for example), select a cookie cutter that is smaller than the diameter of the cheese (about 1¼ inches [3.5 cm] or less).

2. Press the cutter far enough into the cheese to cut through the wax. It's okay if it goes into the cheese a little bit.

3. Remove the cutter from the cheese, and gently pry away the shape you've cut. Often there will be a strip of paper remaining that's used for peeling the wax off the cheese. Using sharp-tipped kitchen scissors, cut through this paper as close to the wax as possible.

Build-It-Yourself Pizza

It can be difficult for a lunch packed at home to compete with the packaged lunches that can be purchased at grocery stores — especially when they're filled with kid-friendly fare like chicken nuggets and pizza. Those lunch kits are loaded with unhealthy, processed food and the portions can be quite small for older children, so tempt your child with a hearty, homemade version that allows him or her to build their own pizza.

INGREDIENTS
Sliced mini pepperoni
Shredded mozzarella cheese
Orange bell pepper
Pizza or pasta sauce
Flatbread such as pita bread
**   or Indian naan**

EQUIPMENT
Two-tier bento box
3 round silicone baking cups
Small, lidded container that will
**   fit inside the bento box**
Kitchen shears
Small spoon for spreading the sauce
**   when eating the lunch**

Variations Just about any topping that's good on pizza will work well for this lunch. Ham, pineapple, sliced olives, and bits of sausage are all delicious.

❶ Place two silicone baking cups filled with the pepperoni and the cheese inside one tier of the bento box.

❷ Cut part of the bell pepper into ¼-inch (6 mm) dice and place in the third silicone cup. Place the cup alongside the pepperoni and cheese.

❸ Fill the lidded container with pizza sauce. Make sure the lid of this container is closed tightly so the sauce does not leak out onto the other items in the box.

❹ Cut the flatbread to fit in the remaining space in the bento box. Hold the bread over the empty space to get an idea of the best place to cut it. Once you've got the basic size right, trim the bread into a round or oval shape so that it resembles a pizza crust. You can also cut it with a round cutter if this is easier.

Butterfly Bento

Lovely butterflies flutter through a tiny garden filled with cheese flowers, fruit, and a simple chicken salad.

INGREDIENTS
Chicken Salad (see recipe below)
Apple
Butterfly crackers
Green grapes
Havarti cheese
Cheddar cheese
Raspberries

EQUIPMENT
Single-tier bento box
Round silicone baking cup
Medium butterfly cutter
Toothpicks
Small flower cutter
Extra-small circle cutter
Flower-stem picks
Fork to eat the salad

Chicken Salad

INGREDIENTS
Cooked chicken, finely chopped
Apple, finely chopped
Celery, finely chopped
Almonds, finely chopped
Mayonnaise

Mix the chicken, apple, celery, and almonds until well combined. Add the mayonnaise to taste and mix well.

❶ Spoon the Chicken Salad (see recipe on this page) into the silicone cup and place it in the top left corner of the bento box.

❷ Cut a thin slice from the side of the apple. Cut a butterfly shape from the slice with a cutter. If desired, use one of the anti-browning techniques on page 65 to keep the apple looking fresh. Place the apple butterfly on top of the Chicken Salad cup.

❸ Stack the butterfly crackers in the lower left-hand corner of the bento box.

❹ Thread three grapes onto each of three toothpicks. Place the grape sticks in a single layer in the upper right corner of the box.

❺ Cut two flower shapes from the Havarti cheese and two small circles from the cheddar. Insert the flower-stem picks into the flower shapes. Place the cheese circles in the middle of the flowers. Put the flowers on top of the grapes.

❻ Fill the remaining space with the raspberries.

Breakfast for Lunch

Having breakfast at lunchtime is a novelty that kids love. Put together some tiny waffle sandwiches, then pair them with a sausage, nuts, and fruit.

INGREDIENTS
½ banana
Blueberries
Glazed walnuts
4 frozen mini waffles (shop bought or homemade)
Peanut butter
Fully cooked chicken apple sausage

EQUIPMENT
Two-tier bento box
Round silicone baking cup

Variations If you don't have mini waffles on hand, a regular waffle cut small will also make a lovely sandwich. You can also skip the waffles altogether and use silver dollar pancakes instead. I often make pancakes on weekends and I'll usually make a few tiny ones to have on hand for later in the week. You can store the pancakes in the fridge for a few days or pop them into a zip-top bag and place them in the freezer for up to a month. To reheat, place them in a toaster oven while they're still frozen and heat until warmed through.

❶ Cut the tip off the banana. Stand the banana on end in one tier of the bento box and cut a chunk of banana the same height as the bento box. Cut a thin slit in the peel of the banana to make it easy to peel and place it back in the box. Reserve the rest of the banana for the waffle filling.

❷ Fill the silicone cup with the blueberries and place it in the same tier as the banana. Fill any remaining space with the glazed walnuts.

❸ Toast the frozen mini waffles according to the package directions, then allow them to cool a bit. If you can avoid putting the waffles in the bento box while they are still warm they are less likely to be soggy at lunchtime.

❹ Spread one mini waffle with peanut butter. Add two or three thin slices of banana, then top with a second mini waffle. Repeat the process to make a second sandwich. Place the sandwiches in the second tier of the bento box.

❺ Cook the sausage in a small skillet until it is just browned. If you are using a fully cooked sausage, you can skip this step, but it does add a bit of flavor to the meat. Slice the sausage, allow it to cool, and put it in the remaining space in the bento box.

Under the Big Top Bento Box

Bring the circus to town (or at least to the lunch table) with this bento box. Your child will feel like she's at the circus when she sees a tent made from fruit, animals balancing on meatballs, and peanuts to snack on while she watches the show. Once she eats the meatballs, she'll find another surprise – a hidden line-up of lions cut from flatbread!

INGREDIENTS
Pineapple
Cantaloupe
Raisins
**Flatbread such as pita bread
or Indian naan**
Small meatballs
Peanuts in their shells

EQUIPMENT
**Single-tier bento box with
three sections**
Small metal flower cutter
Small lion cutter
Circus animal decorative picks

❶ Cut a block of pineapple the same width as the top left section of the bento box, and a third of its length. Remove the core from the pineapple with the flower cutter.

❷ Cut a 1-inch (2.5 cm) thick slice of cantaloupe. Use the flower cutter to cut a piece of cantaloupe to fit into the flower-shape you have cut from the pineapple. This is the door of the circus tent.

❸ Cut 1-inch (2.5 cm) thick triangles of pineapple and cantaloupe and fit them together to make the roof of the tent.

❹ Assemble the circus tent in an upper section of the box, filling any empty spaces at the edges with the raisins.

❺ Cut six lions from the flatbread using the small lion cutter. Fit the lions in the lower section of the bento box, overlapping them slightly.

❻ Place a layer of meatballs on top of the lions. Insert an animal pick into the center of each meatball.

❼ Fill the remaining empty section of the box with the peanuts.

Variations You can swap many kinds of fruit for the pineapple and the cantaloupe. Any kind of melon will work, as will chunks of apples or pears.

Tip If you are having trouble closing the box because the picks are sticking up too far, rotate the meatballs so the picks are lying parallel to the bottom of the box.

Silly Faces Bento Box

When you open this bento box, a whole gang of silly faces smiles up at you. Transform lunchtime favorites – sandwiches, fruit, and celery sticks – with funny googly eyes. So cute and easy!

INGREDIENTS
Sliced whole-wheat bread
Ciliegine (small balls of mozzarella)
Black olives
Tomato
Mayonnaise
Apple
Honey
Mandarin orange
Celery
Peanut butter

EQUIPMENT
Single-tier bento box with inner containers
Medium circle cutter
Toothpick
Icing eyes

Tip *Go crazy with the icing eyes! They can be added to nearly anything and they make a lunch look silly and fun with practically no effort.*

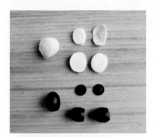

❶ Cut four circles of bread. Cut four slices of ciliegine ⅛ inch (3 mm) thick. You may need to try a few times before you get nice clean slices. Slice the ends off four olives. (Set aside any extra pieces or goof-ups from the cheese and olives to fill the sandwich.) Slice the tomato thinly and cut two small crescent shapes off one of the slices.

❷ Assemble the sandwich filling by placing the tomato slices and scraps of cheese and olives on two of the bread circles.

❸ Assemble the faces on the two other bread circles using ciliegine slices for eyes, olives for pupils, and tomato slivers for mouths, dabbing them with mayonnaise to glue them to the bread. Top the sandwiches with the faces and place them both in one of the larger inner containers of the box.

❹ Cut a wide slab off the side of the apple. Core the rest of the apple and slice it. If desired, use one of the anti-browning techniques on page 65 to keep the apple looking fresh.

❺ Cut the wide slab of apple into two by carving a wavy line across its bottom third. Trim any rough edges on both pieces. Slice the rest of the apple and layer the slices in the bottom of one of the small inner containers. Position the two wavy pieces of apple on top so that the wavy lines create the effect of a mouth. If necessary, trim the sides of the wavy pieces so that they'll fit easily in the container.

❻ Use the toothpick to dab a little honey on the back of two icing eyes. Position the eyes on the top piece of apple to complete the face.

❼ Dab honey on two more icing eyes and place them on the skin of the mandarin orange. Place the orange in the second small inner container.

❽ Cut the celery so that it fits in the remaining inner container. Spread peanut butter on three of the celery sticks, then decorate them with more icing eyes. Place plain celery sticks in the bottom of the container, and then put the decorated ones on top.

Dinosaur Bento Box

Travel back in time to the Jurassic period when salami- and cheese-filled stegosaurs roamed the earth. Include a few broccoli trees and a nest of pretzels for your hard-boiled egg and your favorite kid will feel like a paleontologist – a very hungry paleontologist, that is!

INGREDIENTS
Sliced whole-wheat bread
Sliced cheese
Sliced salami
Desired sandwich condiments
Lettuce leaves for garnish (optional)
Pretzel sticks
Hard-boiled egg
Raw or lightly steamed broccoli

EQUIPMENT
Single-tier bento box divided into three sections
Dinosaur cutter
Kitchen shears
Food-safe marker

Variations Many other sandwich fillings can be used to create the spikes on the dinosaurs' backs—cheese, lettuce, or thinly sliced cucumbers would all work just as well.

❶ Cut four dinosaur shapes from the bread.

❷ Cut two dinosaur shapes from the cheese. Layer the cheese on two of the dinosaur-shaped bread slices, matching up the edges.

❸ Arrange several slices of salami to match the approximate shape of the dinosaur cutter. Cut into two dinosaur shapes. Layer the salami on top of the dinosaur-shaped bread and cheese, matching up the edges.

❹ Cut two slices of salami in half and lay them round side out on the bread, cheese, and salami so they stick out over the edge of the dinosaurs' backs about ½ inch (1.25 cm). Add your desired condiments to the remaining dinosaur-shaped slices of bread and use these slices to top the sandwiches.

❺ Use kitchen shears to cut triangles from the slices of salami that are overhanging the edge of the sandwich, to create a spiky effect.

❻ Layer the lettuce leaves in the largest section of the bento box and place the dinosaur sandwiches on top.

❼ Break the pretzel sticks in half and place in the bottom of one of the remaining sections of the bento box to form a nest for the egg.

❽ Use the food-safe marker to draw dots all over the eggshell. Place the egg on top of the pretzels.

❾ Place the broccoli in the remaining section of the bento box.

Tip The ink in food-safe markers smears easily. Take care not to touch it when you are drawing the dots on the egg or you may get fingerprints all over the place.

Healthy, Homemade Cheese and Crackers

Packaged lunch kits from the grocery store are a popular choice in school cafeterias, but they're not the best choice nutritionally. While cheese and crackers aren't inherently bad, the processed foods in these kits are high in sodium and comprise a long list of unpronounceable ingredients. Make your own version of these lunches by swapping in natural meats and whole-wheat crackers and adding a serving of fruits and veggies.

INGREDIENTS

Whole-wheat crackers
Sliced cheddar cheese
Sliced natural turkey
Clementine wedges
Red bell pepper
Celery

EQUIPMENT

Single-tier bento box
Small flower cutter
Small circle cutter
Square silicone baking cup

❶ Stack up the crackers and put them in the upper left corner of the bento box.

❷ Cut enough flower shapes from the cheese to match the height of the stack of crackers. Place the stack of flowers in the box next to the crackers.

❸ Cut enough circles from the turkey to match the height of the stacks of cheese and crackers. Tuck the stack of turkey into the box next to the cheese.

❹ Pull one slice each of the turkey and the cheese from the stacks and arrange them on top of the stack of crackers.

❺ Fill the silicone cup with the clementines and place it in the box.

❻ Slice the pepper and celery into strips, mix them together, and place them in the remaining space in the bento box.

Rainbow Bento

Let the natural beauty of colorful fruit brighten a cloudy day when you make a rainbow in your child's bento box. A decorated bun and cheerful accessories work to enhance the rainbow theme.

INGREDIENTS
Dinner roll
Berry Lime Fruit Dip (see facing page)
Sliced ham
Raspberries
Cantaloupe chunks
Pineapple chunks
Kiwi chunks

EQUIPMENT
Two-tier bento box
Red, orange, yellow, green, and blue food-safe markers
Rainbow food divider
Small, rainbow-themed sauce container
Flower decorative picks

Tip Food-safe markers work best on smooth surfaces, so when choosing a roll to include in this lunch take a minute to choose one with as few wrinkles on the top as possible.

Berry Lime Fruit Dip

A fruit snack feels like a special dessert when you add a small container of this dip for dunking.

INGREDIENTS
2 oz (55 g) cream cheese, softened to room temperature
5 oz (140 g) berry flavored Greek yogurt
2 teaspoons brown sugar
1 teaspoon lime juice

Combine the cream cheese and yogurt until well blended. Add the brown sugar and lime juice and stir until the sugar dissolves. Serve with the fruit for dipping.

❶ Use the food-safe markers to draw spirals all over the top of the dinner roll. Alternate the color of each spiral to make the roll as bright and cheerful as possible. Put the roll in the larger tier of the bento box. Press the rainbow food divider up against the side of the roll so that the roll will not turn soggy when you put the ham in next to it.

❷ Fill the sauce container with the Berry Lime Fruit Dip and tuck it into the box next to the roll.

❸ Cut the ham into 1-inch (2.5 cm) wide strips and fold them back and forth onto themselves in a wavy pattern. Spear each strip of ham with a flower pick and then spread the strip out evenly along the length of the pick. Place in the space next to the sauce container.

❹ Arrange a row of raspberries along the top edge of the smaller tier of the bento box, following the curve of the box. Follow the curve of the raspberries with the cantaloupe, then the pineapple. Fill in the rest of the space with the kiwi chunks.

Rock 'n' Roll Bento

It's time to get down! A flaming guitar sandwich, a classic LP, and line-up of brightly colored veggies will have any rock 'n' roller screaming for an encore.

INGREDIENTS
Sliced whole-wheat bread
Sliced cheddar cheese
Desired sandwich condiments
Mayonnaise
Black grapes
Grape fruit leather
Baby carrots
Ranch dressing
Sugar snap peas
Grape tomatoes

EQUIPMENT
Single-tier bento box
Guitar cutter
Round silicone baking cup
Medium circle cutter
Paper cut into a 1-inch
   (2.5 cm) circle
Small, lidded container

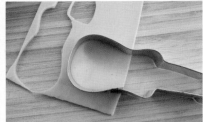

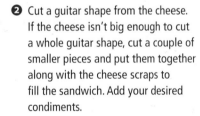

❶ Cut two guitar shapes from the bread.

❷ Cut a guitar shape from the cheese. If the cheese isn't big enough to cut a whole guitar shape, cut a couple of smaller pieces and put them together along with the cheese scraps to fill the sandwich. Add your desired condiments.

❸ Cut a smaller piece of cheese with the wider end of the guitar cutter. Using the tip of a sharp knife, cut the cheese to resemble flames. Place the flame cutout on top of the sandwich, gluing it to the bread with a little mayonnaise. Place the sandwich in the box.

❹ Fill the silicone cup with the black grapes and place it in the lower right corner of the bento box.

❺ To make the record, cut four circles from the fruit leather and stack them on top of each other. A single layer will be too floppy, but stacking them gives the piece a bit of structure. Write a song and band name on the piece of paper. Place the paper in the center of the fruit leather to act as the record's label. Place the fruit-leather record on top of the grapes.

❻ Stand the carrots on end and tuck them into the upper right corner of the bento box.

❼ Fill the small, lidded container with the ranch dressing or another dipping sauce and place it in the space above the guitar sandwich.

❽ Cut the sugar snap peas to the same height as the box and then use them to fill the space above the guitar.

❾ Fill the last bit of empty space with the grape tomatoes.

Space Bento Box

Blast into outer space and explore this out of this world lunch! You'll find sun and moon sandwiches, grape planets, and billions and billions of stars made from cookies and crackers.

INGREDIENTS

Sliced sourdough bread
Sliced cheddar cheese
Sandwich condiments
Sliced turkey
Grapes
Blueberries
Space-themed crackers
Star-shaped cookies

EQUIPMENT

Single-tier bento box with inner containers
Medium circle cutter
Small rocket ship cutter
Small star cutter
Flying saucer or other space-themed decorative pick

❶ Cut four circles from the bread.

❷ Lay one of the bread circles on a slice of cheese and cut a square the same size as the diameter of the bread circle. Repeat with a second slice of cheese.

❸ Place the two slices of cheese on one of the bread circles, offsetting them so that they form a star. Add your desired condiments then top with another of the bread circles, taking care to hide additional items underneath the bread. Place the sandwich in the box.

❹ Cut a small rocket ship and a star from the leftover cheese.

❺ Sometimes it can be difficult to remove cheese from a small cutter with your fingers. If this happens, gently ease the piece of cheese out of the cutter with the tip of your knife (a toothpick also works well)

taking care not to mark the cheese too much.

❻ Cut circles from the turkey using the same cutter you used to cut the bread. The turkey circles don't need to be perfectly shaped, but using the cutter will ensure the meat doesn't stick out of the sides of the bread.

❼ Layer any leftover cheese scraps on the third circle of bread along with the turkey and condiments. Top with the last circle of bread, then place the rocket ship and star-shaped pieces of cheese on top of the sandwich and put it in the box.

❽ Thread grapes onto the flying saucer pick. Place more grapes in an inner container and put the grape skewer on top.

❾ Fill any remaining spaces in the box with the blueberries, space-themed crackers, and star-shaped cookies.

Star Wars Bento Box

Pay homage to everyone's favorite space saga with a lunch that pits the dark side against a Jedi master. A few purchased pieces of equipment – a plunger cookie-cutter, light saber picks, and a Darth Vader ring – help this bento come together quickly. Two small orange moons nestled in the darkness of blueberry space add to the ambience.

INGREDIENTS

2 mandarin oranges, peeled
Blueberries
Sliced, soft whole-wheat bread
Desired sandwich fillings and condiments
Pretzel sticks
Sliced cucumber
Mozzarella cheese stick

EQUIPMENT

Single-tier bento box with divider
Yoda plunger cutter
Darth Vader ring
Light saber decorative picks

Variations Star Wars party supplies are easily found online, but if you are unable to locate them you can add Star Wars imagery to a bento box in other ways. Thread raspberries or green grapes onto a toothpick or wooden skewer to emulate a light saber, or add Star Wars stickers to a decorative pick to customize it.

❶ Position the bento box divider near one end of the box. Place the mandarin oranges in the smaller section and fill in the gaps around them with the blueberries.

❷ Use the plunger cutter to cut a shape from a slice of bread. With the bread still in the cutter, press down as hard as you can on the plunger to make the impression of Yoda's face. The bread will be very thin after you stamp it. If it sticks to the cutter, peel it off carefully to avoid tearing the bread. Cut another shape from the slice of bread to use for the bottom of the sandwich. Don't stamp this layer—it will be invisible once it's in the box and the thicker piece of bread will help give the sandwich structure. Repeat the cutting and stamping process to make a second sandwich. Fill the sandwiches with your desired ingredients then stack them on top of each other in the upper right corner of the bento box.

❸ Layer the pretzel sticks in the bento box between the divider and the sandwiches. If necessary, break some of the pretzels so that they'll fit without overlapping each other.

❹ Fill the remaining space with the sliced cucumber.

❺ If the cheese stick is wrapped, remove the wrapping. Slide the cheese stick through the finger hole of the Darth Vader ring. Place it on top of the pretzels in the box.

❻ Arrange the light saber picks in a criss-cross pattern on top of the cucumbers.

Superstar Bento Box

Stars are one of the most versatile shapes in a cookie-cutter collection. The shape is easy to find and available in just about every size. It appeals to both boys and girls, and even adults who shy away from cutesy bento boxes don't mind a few stars in their lunches. Give this shape the … er … superstar treatment with this fun meal.

INGREDIENTS
Sliced white bread
Desired sandwich fillings
Cucumber
Red bell pepper piece
Yellow bell pepper piece
Super Quick Pasta Salad (see
facing page)

EQUIPMENT
Two-tier bento box
Medium, small, and extra-small
star cutters
Star-shaped silicone baking cup
Spoon or fork to eat with

❶ Cut four medium-sized stars from the bread. Use the stars to make two sandwiches with the fillings of your choice. Place the sandwiches in one tier of the bento box.

❷ Slice the cucumber thinly. Use the small star cutter to cut several star shapes from the slices. Chop the cucumber scraps into bite-sized pieces, place in the bottom of the star-shaped cup, and then top with the cucumber stars. Put the cup into the box next to the sandwiches.

❸ Peel the red and yellow bell pepper pieces, then cut them into star shapes with the smallest star cutter. Chop the remaining bell pepper into ¼-inch (6 mm) dice and set aside to make the Super Quick Pasta Salad (see facing page).

❹ Fill the second tier of the box with the Super Quick Pasta Salad and sprinkle the bell pepper stars on top.

Super Quick Pasta Salad

This salad comes together in a flash with leftover pasta and fresh veggies from the fridge. I've used bell peppers here, but tomatoes, zucchini, carrots, or broccoli would all be fine choices.

INGREDIENTS

½ **cup (30 g) cooked stelline or other small pasta**

½ **cup (75 g) diced bell pepper (¼-inch [6 mm] dice)**

Bottled vinaigrette

Mix the stelline pasta and bell pepper together. Add the vinaigrette to taste, and mix well.

Choo-Choo Train Bento

All aboard! The train is leaving the station for lunch! This cheery choo-choo train bento box comes complete with pretzel train tracks, a tiny suitcase full of peaches, and a box car full of veggies to enjoy. Tickets please!

INGREDIENTS

Canned peaches
Sprinkles
Sugar snap peas
Celery
Veggie Cream Cheese (see facing page)
Grape tomatoes
Sliced whole-wheat bread
Desired sandwich fillings
Sliced cheddar cheese
Pretzel sticks

EQUIPMENT

Two-tier bento box
Lidded, suitcase-shaped silicone cup
Train cutter
Small circle cutter
Extra-small circle cutter
Extra-small star cutter

Tip Canned peaches are convenient to have on hand for days when the fruit bowl is empty, but they can be high in sugar. To reduce the sugar, drain off the syrup and rinse the peaches under running water. Let them sit in the strainer for a few minutes and blot them with a paper towel to remove as much moisture as possible before packing them in the bento box. This will prevent them from making the whole lunch soggy.

❶ Rinse and drain the peaches, then place them in the suitcase cup. Scatter a few sprinkles on top, put the lid on the cup, and place it in one tier of the bento box.

❷ Cut the sugar snap peas in half and stand them on end next to the suitcase cup.

❸ Cut the celery to fit in the box. Spread the Veggie Cream Cheese on the celery sticks and place them in the space next to the peas.

❹ Fill the last bit of space in the tier with the tomatoes.

❺ Cut two engine shapes from the bread with the train cutter. To make the coal tender, cut two rectangles from another slice of bread, then position the train cutter on them in such a way that it cuts out wheels but doesn't cut out any of the other parts of the train. Fill the sandwiches and place them in the second tier of the bento box.

❻ Use the circle and star cutters and a knife to cut decorations for the sandwiches from the cheese. Place the decorations on top of the sandwiches.

❼ Tuck a few pretzel sticks below the sandwiches to suggest train tracks. Place a celery stick in the space above the coal tender to keep the sandwiches from moving around while the lunch is in transit.

Veggie Cream Cheese

This dip is delicious spread on celery sticks or toast or sandwiched between crackers. It's also a great way to use up the scraps generated when cutting vegetables into shapes. If you don't have carrot or bell pepper on hand, experiment with other vegetables such as sugar snap peas or broccoli.

INGREDIENTS
4 oz (115 g) less fat cream cheese, softened
¼ teaspoon garlic powder
½ teaspoon dried dill
1½ tablespoons finely chopped carrot
1½ tablespoons finely chopped red bell pepper

Mix all the ingredients in a bowl until evenly combined.

EXTRA-
SPECIAL
BENTOS

Ballerina Bento Box

Your tiny dancer will feel like a prima ballerina when she opens this bento box packed with ballet-slipper sandwiches, watermelon hearts, and a bouquet of radish roses.

INGREDIENTS

Sliced whole-wheat bread
Thinly sliced ham
Mayonnaise
Desired condiments
Watermelon
Radishes

EQUIPMENT

Single-tier bento box
Templates (see page 120)
Pink bow decorative picks
Small heart cutter
Heart-shaped silicone baking cup

HOW TO MAKE RADISH ROSES

1. Wash and trim your radish by cutting off the root and stem ends.

2. With a sharp knife, carefully cut the edge of the radish about ¾ of the way to the bottom. Continue making small cuts around the edge of the radish, as shown, to make petals.

3. If you like, make another set of small cuts in a circle around the inside of the radish.

4. Soak the radish in a small bowl of water overnight until the edges open up and the radish has "bloomed."

5. Remove the radish from the bowl, pat dry with a paper towel, and add it to your bento box!

❶ Lay the full template (see page 120) on top of the bread and cut around it with kitchen shears to make four ballet-slipper shapes.

❷ Lay the small template on a piece of ham and cut out with a sharp knife. Lay the ham on top of one of the slipper-shaped pieces of bread. Spread a little mayonnaise on the back of the ham to glue it to the bread so it stays in place. Repeat to make another piece.

❸ Cut "ribbons" from the ham using the template, and arrange on the two decorated pieces of bread.

❹ Cut the remaining scraps of ham to fit inside the sandwich and place on top of the two remaining slipper-shaped pieces of bread along with any other desired sandwich fillings and condiments. Top with the decorated slices of bread, then spear with a bow-shaped decorative pick to keep the sandwich from coming apart while eating. Place the sandwiches in the bento box.

❺ Cut a ¼-inch (6 mm) thick slice of watermelon. Cut hearts from the watermelon using the cutter. Place the hearts in the silicone cup and place it next to the sandwiches.

❻ Fill the remaining space with the radishes and a radish "rose" (see this page for instructions).

Little Car Bento

A little egg car drives past some houses under a blueberry sky in this cute bento box.

INGREDIENTS
Hard-boiled egg
Wheat crackers
Celery
Sliced cheese
Blueberries

EQUIPMENT
Single-tier bento box
Liquid food coloring
Car-shaped egg mold
Small house cutter

❶ Fill a bowl with enough water to cover the egg and add several drops of liquid food coloring.

❷ Peel the egg and let it soak in the dye until it has reached the desired color.

❸ Form the egg into the shape of a car using the egg mold (see instructions on page 77).

❹ Begin to assemble the bento box by standing the wheat crackers upright along the bottom edge of the box. (This will be the "road" for the car to drive on.)

❺ Cut the celery into sticks and arrange in one half of the box above the crackers.

❻ Start cutting house shapes from the cheese and placing them on top of crackers. Build two stacks of cheese and crackers in the space above the celery sticks. Stop when the stacks reach the top edge of the box.

❼ Place the car-shaped egg in the box in the space to the right of the celery sticks. Make sure to pat it with a paper towel before putting it in the box to absorb any excess moisture that might make the crackers soggy.

❽ Fill the remaining space in the box with the blueberries.

Puppy Dog

This doggie sandwich will greet you with a friendly smile and a wagging tail at lunchtime. He comes complete with several doggie accessories: a pile of bones, a bowl of blueberry "water," and a fire hydrant too!

INGREDIENTS

Sliced white bread
Sliced ham
Desired sandwich fillings and condiments
Sliced pumpernickel bread
Mayonnaise
Blueberries
Red bell pepper
Dog-bone Pita Chips (see facing page)

EQUIPMENT

Single-tier bento box
Large circle cutter
Small circle cutter
Drinking glass or rolling pin
Extra-small oval cutter
Extra-small triangle cutter
Extra-small crescent cutter
Round silicone baking cup
Bone-shaped cutter
Fire-hydrant cutter
Dog-shaped food divider (optional)

Tip If you don't have a circle cutter exactly the size you need, you probably have one hiding in your cupboards! Mugs, glasses, bowls, and jars can all be used to cut circles for your bento creations.

❶ Cut two large circles from the white bread. This will be the base of the dog sandwich. Cut a few circles of ham using the same cutter and fill the sandwich with the ham and any other desired fillings or condiments. Cut a small oval from one of the ham scraps to use for the dog's tongue and clip the end off to make a straight edge.

❷ Cut another, smaller circle from the pumpernickel bread. Cut an American football shape by positioning the edge of the cutter in the middle of the circle. Cut another American football shape using the second half of the bread circle. These will be the ears.

❸ Flatten a small piece of pumpernickel bread by rolling a drinking glass over it. (You can also use a rolling pin, or even just lean on it and flatten it with the palm of your hand.) Cut two small ovals for the eyes, a small triangle for

the nose, and a small crescent for the mouth. Arrange the ears near the top of the bread so they overhang the edge a bit, spreading the backs with a little mayonnaise to help glue them down. Add the other pieces to make a face as shown in the photo. Carefully place the sandwich at the far end of the bento box.

❹ Fill the silicone cup with blueberries and place it in the lower left hand corner of the box.

❺ Cut the bell pepper into large chunks, peel them, and cut out a few fire-hydrant shapes. Cut any scraps into strips and put them in the lower right corner of the box. Cover the scraps with the fire hydrants.

❻ Fill the remaining space with Dog-bone Pita Chips (see facing page).

Dog-bone Pita Chips

INGREDIENTS
1 pita bread
2 teaspoons butter
½ teaspoon cinnamon
½ teaspoon sugar

❶ Preheat oven to 350ºF (175ºC).

❷ Split the bread horizontally into two rounds. Spread the rough side of each round with the butter. Mix the cinnamon and the sugar and sprinkle over the bread. Cut the bread into dog-bone shapes with a cookie cutter or shears.

❸ Put the shapes on an ungreased cookie sheet, butter side up. Bake for 7–9 minutes until golden brown. Let cool before putting them in the bento box.

On the Farm

Moooo! Cluck cluck! Oink! With a cow, chicken, a couple of pigs, and farm fresh produce this lunch is ready to go on a field trip to a farm or a petting zoo.

INGREDIENTS
Carrot
Hard-boiled egg
Sliced apple
Frozen corn
Grape tomatoes
Cooked green beans
Harvarti cheese
Sliced white bread
Sliced deli ham
Desired sandwich fillings and condiments
Cooked and shelled edamame

EQUIPMENT
Single-tier divided bento box
Extra-small flower cutter
Black food-safe marker
Pig-shaped silicone baking cup
Small cow cutter
Pig stamping-cutter
Spoon to eat with

❶ Cut two thin rounds from the carrot and cut a small flower from one piece and a small triangle from the other. Peel the hard-boiled egg and cut a slit in the pointed end with the tip of a sharp knife. Insert the carrot flower to make the rooster's comb. Cut another small, horizontal slit about halfway down the side of the egg and insert the carrot triangle to make the beak. Draw eyes on the egg with the food marker and place the decorated egg in the upper right section of the bento box.

❷ Fill the space next to the egg with sliced apple. If desired, use one of the anti-browning techniques on page 65 to keep the apple looking fresh.

❸ Fill the pig cup with the corn and place in the lower left section of the box. Fill the remaining space in the section with the tomatoes.

❹ Place the green beans in the upper left section of the box, trimming them to fit.

❺ Cut a cow shape from the cheese. Add an eye and a few spots with the food marker and place it on top of the green beans.

❻ Use the outer piece of the pig cutter to cut two pig head shapes from the bread. Stamp one of the pieces of bread to make a pig face. Cut a pig head shape from the ham. Use the cutting side of the pig plate to cut out the pig's facial features. Place the ears, eyes, and snout on top of the stamped slice of bread, gluing them down with mayonnaise. Fill the sandwich with another pig-shaped piece of ham, the ham scraps, and any other fillings and place it in the last empty section in the bento box.

❼ Fill the empty space around the sandwich with the edamame.

Building Bricks Bento Box

Young engineers will adore this homage to their favorite building brick. Though this bento is a bit fussier than most, the techniques used to create it — mostly just cutting circles and rectangles — are easy once you get the hang of them.

INGREDIENTS
Cantaloupe
Sliced whole-wheat bread
Sliced cheddar cheese
Mayonnaise
Desired sandwich fillings and condiments
Large carrot
Cucumber
Ranch dressing

EQUIPMENT
Two-tier building-brick bento box
**Drinking straw, cut to a 2-inch (5 cm)
    length**
Toothpick
Small circle cutter
Small building-brick sauce container

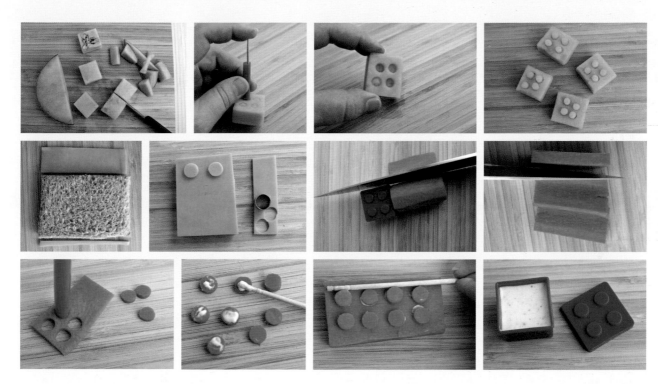

1. Cut a 1-inch (2.5 cm) thick slice of cantaloupe, then cut four 1-inch (2.5 cm) cubes from the slice. Position the straw perpendicular to the topside of the cantaloupe cube and gently push the straw all the way through it. Remove the straw from the cantaloupe and gently push out the piece of cantaloupe inside the straw using a toothpick, being careful to keep it whole. Repeat until you have pierced each cantaloupe cube four times. Do your best to space the cuts evenly.

2. Flip a cantaloupe cube over and gently reinsert the cantaloupe cylinders, pressing on them with the toothpick until they are sticking out of the top about ⅛ inch (3 mm). Repeat to make four cantaloupe bricks and place them in the bottom of one of the tiers of the bento box.

3. Cut the crusts off a slice of bread to form a rectangle. Cut the rectangle in half. Using one of the bread pieces as a guide, trim a slice of cheese so that it matches the shape of the bread. Cut six small circles from the cheese scraps and glue them with mayonnaise onto the cheese to mimic the studs on a building brick. Fill the sandwich, top it with the cheese brick, and place it in the bento box next to the cantaloupe bricks.

4. Cut a chunk from the carrot. Using the sauce container as a guide, peel and trim the carrot so that it's basically square. Most of the carrot will be hidden from view so it doesn't have to be perfect, but try to cut right angles on at least one side so that it mimics the sharp corners of a building brick. Reserve the scraps.

5. Slice the carrot square into planks to make it easier to eat. Stack the planks up, with the best-looking slice on top.

6. Use the drinking straw to cut eight small circles from one of your carrot scraps. Dab a small amount of mayonnaise on the back of each circle and then place them on top of your carrot. Use the toothpick to straighten the lines. If you smear mayonnaise on the carrot, you can use the tip of the toothpick to scrape it off.

7. Repeat this process to make two more carrot bricks and three cucumber bricks. Place the bricks in the second tier of the bento box.

8. Fill the sauce container with the dressing. Tuck into the second tier of the bento box.

Cat and Mouse Bento

The mice eat the cheese and the cats chase the mice! Adding some playful cats and a handful of cute strawberry mice to your bento box makes lunchtime special. A chunk of tasty Swiss cheese riddled with holes helps achieve that classic cartoon effect.

INGREDIENTS
Small chunk Swiss cheese
Strawberries
Sliced almonds
Honey
Fruit leather
Flatbread
Sliced deli turkey

EQUIPMENT
Two-tier bento box
Small metal measuring spoon
Triangle-shaped silicone baking cup
Icing eyes
Extra-small circle cutter or drinking straw
Small cat cutter

❶ Cut the Swiss cheese into a triangle shape. If your cheese doesn't have many holes, you can use a small metal measuring spoon to scoop out small divots of cheese for a quintessential "cheesy" look. Put the cheese in the silicone cup and place it in a corner of one of the tiers of the box.

❷ To make a strawberry mouse, hull a strawberry and cut it in half lengthwise. Cut two small horizontal slits at the wide end of the strawberry. Insert sliced almonds for the ears. Attach icing eyes under the almonds, using a dab of honey as glue. Finally, cut a small circle from the fruit leather for the nose and attach it near the tip of the strawberry. Repeat this process to make two more mice.

❸ Slice a few strawberries into ¼-inch (6 mm) slices and arrange in a double layer next to the cheese. Place the strawberry mice on top.

❹ Cut the flatbread to fit inside the second tier of the bento box. Slice it into four equal pieces and place in the box.

❺ Stack two slices of turkey and fold them in half. Cut a four-layered cat shape from the stack. Repeat three times. Place one cat on each of the four slices of bread.

Under the Sea Bento

Octopuses made from hot dog are a classic Japanese bento box preparation. If you put a pot of water on to boil when you start making this lunch the water should be ready to cook the hot dog as you finish cutting it. Seeing the tentacles curl up in the pot is surprisingly fun. Round out the lunch with some kiwi sea stars, a school of carrot fish, and whale-tail tortilla chips.

INGREDIENTS
Cucumber
1 hot dog
1 kiwi
Large carrot
Blue corn tortilla chips

EQUIPMENT
Single-tier divided bento box
Paring knife
Medium and small star cutters
Kitchen shears
Vegetable peeler

Tip If you have a spare minute, cut the hot dog tentacles to sharp points. This helps them curl up a bit more and makes the hot dog look more octopus-like.

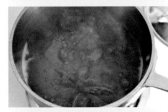

❶ Cut a chunk of cucumber slightly shorter than the width of the biggest section of the bento box. Slice the cucumber in half lengthwise. With a sharp paring knife, cut out the center of the cucumber, leaving about ⅛ inch (3 mm) of flesh on the skin.

❷ Flatten the cucumber skin with the palm of your hand, taking care not to crack it. (This should be easy if the skin is not too thick.) Cut the cucumber to look like seaweed using a pair of sharp kitchen shears. Place the "seaweed" in the biggest section of the bento box.

❸ Cut the hot dog in half crosswise. Starting a third of the way from the round end of one piece of hot dog, cut lengthwise to the end, making two "legs." Repeat the process to cut the two legs in half to make four legs, then the four legs in half to make eight.

❹ Cook the two pieces of hot dog in a pan of boiling water for 1–2 minutes or until the tentacles curl a little. Drain well on a paper towel, and then place on top of the cucumber seaweed in the bento box.

❺ Cut the kiwi into ¼-inch (6 mm) slices, and then cut the slices into star shapes with the cutters. Trim any peel off the corners of the kiwi stars and place in them the upper right section of the bento box.

❻ Cut and peel a 2-inch (5 cm) chunk from the widest end of the carrot. Use the vegetable peeler to cut long thin strips from the carrot chunk. Use a paring knife to cut fish shapes from the strips. Place them in the lower left section of the box.

❼ Finally, place the tortilla chips in the remaining empty area of the box.

Pretty Princess Bento Box

Send your sweet little princess to school with this royal bento lunch featuring a bejeweled crown, a magic wand, and vegetable frogs.

INGREDIENTS
Sliced whole-wheat
  bread
Cream cheese
Sliced cucumber
Green bell pepper piece
Cereal bar
Strawberries
Carrot

EQUIPMENT
Two-tier bento box
Crown cutter
Jewel decorative picks
Frog cutter
Star cutter

❶ Cut two crowns from the bread using the cutter. Spread cream cheese on one of the crowns. Arrange the sliced cucumber in a shape close to that of the crown cutter. Cut a crown from the sliced cucumber and transfer it to the piece of bread spread with cream cheese. Arrange the cucumber so it matches up with the edges of the bread.

❷ Top the sandwich with the second bread crown. Spear the sandwich with the jewel decorative picks and place in one tier of the bento box.

❸ Peel the piece of green bell pepper and press it out flat on a work surface. Cut frog shapes from the bell pepper and from the remaining sliced cucumber. Layer the vegetable scraps

along the far side of the other tier of the bento box, then layer the frog shapes on top.

❹ Cut the cereal bar to fit in the space below the frogs and tuck into the box.

❺ Cut a ¼-inch (6 mm) slice from one of the largest strawberries. Cut a star shape from the slice using the cutter. Cut a matchstick shape from the carrot. Cut a slit in the side of the strawberry star and insert the end of the carrot into the hole to make a magic wand. Place the wand on top of the cereal bar.

❻ Chop the remaining strawberries into small pieces and use them to fill in the empty spaces surrounding the sandwich.

Robot Bento Box

Beep! Boop! Beep! The robots are here with your lunch! Convert a hot dog to a robot friend with a few cuts of a knife. A decorated dinner roll, grapes, and edamame complete the menu.

INGREDIENTS
Turkey hot dog
Small slice Swiss, muenster, or other white cheese
Ketchup or mustard
Dinner roll
Cooked and shelled edamame
Grapes

EQUIPMENT
Two-tier bento box
Extra-small circle cutter
Dry spaghetti
Black, red, green, and blue food-safe marker
Small sauce container
Robot rubber stamp
Robot decorative pick
Square silicone baking cup

Tip *Rubber stamps designed for crafting can create a fun look in a bento box, but be careful not to mix crafting ink with food-safe ink. Use stamps purchased for bentos exclusively for food preparation and carefully wash them before and after each use.*

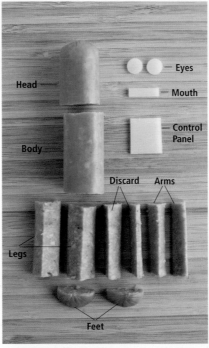

❶ Cut the hot dog crosswise into three pieces, making the top piece slightly shorter and the bottom piece slightly longer than the middle piece. Cut the round tip off the bottom of the longest piece and then cut the tip in half to use for the robot's feet. Cut the remaining part of the longest piece into quarters from end to end. Two of these quarters will be used for the robot's legs. Discard one of the quarters, then cut the remaining quarter in half lengthwise to make the robot's arms.

❷ From the slice of cheese cut two small circles for eyes, a thin rectangle for the mouth, and a square for the control panel.

❸ Assemble the robot using pieces of dry spaghetti to connect the head and limbs to the body piece and the feet to the legs. Carefully move the robot to the smaller tier of the bento box.

❹ Use the food-safe markers to add black dots to the cheese eyes. Place the eyes and mouth on the robot's head to make a face. Add colored dots to the cheese control panel and position it on the robot's chest.

❺ Fill the small sauce container with ketchup or mustard and place it beneath the robot.

❻ Make sure the robot stamp is very clean, and then quickly go over the entire image with the blue food marker. Stamp the image onto the dinner roll. Place the roll in the second tier of the box.

❼ Thread some edamame onto the robot pick. Put the pick in the square cup, fill the empty space around the pick with more edamame, and place the cup in the second tier of the box.

❽ Fill the empty space between the dinner roll and the edamame with the grapes.

Snow White and the Seven Dwarfs Bento Box

An evil queen was jealous of a beautiful girl named Snow White. Snow White ran away to live in a bento box with seven dwarfs (actually sandwiches and fruit on jewel picks) until the queen tried to poison her with an apple. But the apple was merely delicious, not deadly, and they lived happily ever after ... until a hungry child ate everyone. The end.

INGREDIENTS
1 Babybel cheese
Red apple
Sliced whole-wheat bread
Sliced muenster cheese
Sliced roast beef
Grainy mustard
Green grapes
Clementine wedges

EQUIPMENT
Single-tier bento box
Red and black food-safe markers
1 bow decorative pick
Small flower cutter
7 jewel decorative picks

WORKING WITH FOOD-SAFE MARKERS

Follow the easy tips below to make sure you get the best out of these useful tools:

1. *Food-safe markers work best on dry surfaces such as bread, crackers, and other baked goods. If you use them on damp foods such as cheese or tofu, first blot the food with a paper towel to remove excess moisture.*

2. *If the ink doesn't flow easily from the marker, try pressing down with the tip to make small dots rather than using longer strokes. Blot the marker frequently on a paper towel while making your design to wipe crumbs or excess moisture from the marker tip and let the ink flow more freely.*

3. *Be sure to clean your markers to remove food residue before putting them away. Food left on the tip can spoil, and ruin the marker.*

4. *Food-safe markers are kitchen tools and ultimately their ink will be consumed. Keep the markers clean and store them in the refrigerator to prolong their shelf life.*

❶ Use a sharp knife to carve the outline of Snow White's hair in the wax of the Babybel cheese. Gently pull the wax cutout off the cheese taking care not to rip the "hair." There will be a thin strip of paper left behind. Cut it with the scissors as close to the wax as you can. If a little bit of paper remains after cutting, tuck it under the wax "hair" with the tip of your knife to hide it.

❷ Use the food-safe markers to draw eyes and a mouth on the cheese. Add the bow

pick near the top of the cheese. Place the cheese in the lower right corner of the box.

❸ Cut one large slab from the apple, and cut the rest of apple into slices. Cut a "bite" out of the large slab by putting half of the flower cutter over the edge. Place the plain slices of apple in the upper left corner of the box, then place the decorated slab of apple on top.

❹ Trim the bread into a rectangle, then cut the rectangle into six equal pieces. Cut

the cheese and meat into squares the same size as the bread, then use them to assemble the mini sandwiches along with a little mustard until you have three sandwich kebabs. Spear each kebab with a jewel pick and place in the lower left corner of the bento box.

❺ Assemble four fruit kebabs on the remaining jewel picks with a grape and a few wedges of clementine on each one. Use the fruit skewers to fill the remaining space in the bento box.

Hip to Be Square

You don't need a bunch of special equipment to make a pretty bento box, and this lunch is an excellent example of how you can create a gorgeous, decorative meal using nothing other than a sharp kitchen knife. Cut and cube sweet potato, chicken, and apple, add some cheese and crackers, and treat yourself to a beautiful lunch. For an extra flourish, decorate your bento box with a homemade flag!

INGREDIENTS
Baked sweet potato
Roasted chicken breast
Red apple
Sliced cheddar cheese
Mini saltine crackers

EQUIPMENT
Two-tier bento box
2 square silicone baking cups
Flag decorative picks (see facing page)

Tip *It's simple to cook a sweet potato in the microwave! Wash the potato, prick it all over with a fork, place on a plate to collect any juice that escapes while cooking, then microwave it on high for 5–10 minutes until it's easily pierced with a fork.*

EXTRA-SPECIAL BENTOS

❶ Place two square silicone cups side by side in one tier of the bento box.

❷ Peel the potato, cut it into even cubes, and arrange the cubes neatly in one of the cups.

❸ Cut the chicken breast into cubes and arrange those neatly in the second cup. Insert a flag pick (see facing page) into one of the cubes of chicken.

❹ Cut the apple into large wedges. Cut a grid pattern into the largest piece with a knife, taking care to just barely cut through the skin.

Slide the tip of the knife under alternate squares of the apple skin and pop them off. Be sure to treat the apple with one of the anti-browning methods described on the facing page so that it stays pretty until lunchtime. Place the apple in the second tier of the bento box.

❺ Cut the sliced cheddar cheese into squares that are just a little smaller than the mini saltine crackers. Stack the cheese and crackers in a square grid in the remaining space in the bento box.

Flag Picks

EQUIPMENT
Scissors
Washi tape
Toothpicks

Cut a piece of tape about 1½ inches (4 cm) long. Lay the tape sticky side up and place the blunt end of the toothpick in the center, perpendicular to the long edge. Fold the tape over onto itself, pressing it tightly around the toothpick. Trim the tape into a square with the scissors.

HOW TO KEEP APPLES (AND OTHER FRUIT) FROM BROWNING

There's nothing quite so disappointing as opening up your bento box to find brown, mushy apple slices. Keep apples fresh and white using one of these methods:

1. *Fruit Fresh—Sprinkle this product on your apple slices to keep them looking fresh all day. I've found that this product works better than any other technique to prevent apples from browning.*

2. *Pineapple juice—A quick dip in this sweet juice also keeps apples from oxidizing. If you don't have bottled pineapple juice on hand, the juice from canned pineapple works well.*

3. *Water with a little lemon juice—Let the apple soak in water with a little lemon juice for about 5 minutes then pat dry and put it in the bento box. Be careful not to add too much lemon to the water or the apple will taste sour.*

4. *Crushed vitamin C tablet dissolved in water—In a pinch you can raid your vitamin bottle, crush a tablet with the back of a spoon, and mix it up with water. Dip in the apple, dry well, and pack.*

Superhero Bento

It's a bird! It's a plane! It's Captain Bento! He's famous for his sandwich mask and for his tortilla lightning bolts that curb hunger in just a few bites. His sidekicks, super oranges and tomatoes, give junior heroes extra strength to make it through the day.

INGREDIENTS
Sliced white bread
Desired sandwich fillings and
    condiments
Sliced cheddar cheese
Fruit leather
Mandarin orange wedges
Grape tomatoes
Lightning-bolt tortilla chips (see
    recipe on this page)

EQUIPMENT
Single-tier bento box with inner
    containers
Mask template (see page 120)
Extra-small star cutter
Star-shaped silicone baking cup

❶ Cut out the mask template (see page 120), lay it on the bread, and cut around it. Repeat to cut a second mask shape from the bread. Use the mask-shaped bread to assemble a sandwich with your desired filling. Cut another mask shape, from the cheese, this time making eye holes. Tuck any leftover scraps of cheese inside your sandwich. Put the cheese mask on top of the sandwich and place it in one of the larger inner containers.

❷ Cut a small star shape from the fruit leather and place it in the middle of the cheese mask for decoration. You can tuck the remaining fruit leather into the silverware tray of the bento box if you want.

❸ Place a handful of the mandarin orange wedges in the bottom of one of the smaller inner containers. Arrange the rest of the wedges on top in two vertical columns, tilting the outside corners up a little to suggest flames.

❹ Fill the star-shaped cup with the tomatoes and place in the other small inner container.

❺ Put the lightning-bolt chips in the remaining container.

Homemade Tortilla Chips

These tortilla chips are quick to make and lower in oil than store-bought chips. They're great for bento boxes as you can cut them into shapes to match your theme. I used kitchen shears to make the shapes, but cookie cutters work well too.

INGREDIENTS
Flour tortillas
Spray oil
Salt

Preheat the oven to 350ºF (175ºC). Cut the tortillas into lightning bolts and spread in a single layer on a cookie sheet, taking care not to overlap the pieces. Spray the pieces with oil and sprinkle with salt. Bake for 8–10 minutes or until lightly browned and crisp.

Rainbow Bento Box for a Toddler

Very young children aren't as likely to appreciate an artfully packed lunch as older children might be, but they still benefit from having naturally colorful foods presented attractively. Pack a lunch with a rainbow of veggies and a happy rice "cloud" to entice them to try new flavors. Be sure to chop the food into small pieces to avoid choking hazards and so that little fingers can easily pick up the food.

INGREDIENTS
Cooked rice
Small sheet nori seaweed
Cherry tomatoes
Steamed baby carrots
Corn
Peas
Ham
Cheerios

EQUIPMENT
Two-tier bento box
Blue food coloring
Star-shaped rice mold
Nori face punch
2 round silicone baking cups

Variations *Create the rainbow in this box using fruit instead of vegetables. Choose chopped strawberries, cantaloupe, pineapple, and kiwi or refer to the list of foods by color on page 11 for more inspiration.*

❶ While the rice is still warm, add a few drops of food coloring and stir well until the rice is an even shade of light blue. Begin with two drops and add a single drop at a time until the desired color is achieved.

❷ Pack the rice tightly into the rice mold. Close the lid and then place the mold in the refrigerator until cool. This step can be completed the night before. Reserve any leftover rice for another use.

❸ When the rice has cooled, remove it from the mold. Use the face punch to cut two eyes and a mouth from a sheet of nori. Arrange them on the rice ball (see instructions on page 76). Place the rice ball to the right side of one of the tiers of the bento box.

❹ Cut the tomatoes into small dice. Chop the carrots into small pieces. Defrost the corn and peas by running them under warm water.

❺ Position the internal lid for the top tier of the bento box (or another thin, flexible piece of plastic) about a quarter of the way down from the top of the tier where you've placed the rice ball. Fill the space with the chopped tomatoes.

❻ Carefully remove the lid and reposition it so it divides the box in half horizontally. Fill the space between the lid and the tomatoes with the carrot pieces and again remove the plastic carefully from the box.

❼ Position the lid a quarter of the distance from the bottom of the box and fill the space between the lid and the carrots with the corn. Slowly remove the lid and fill the remaining space in the box with the peas. If a little corn falls down when you pull the lid out, don't worry—just put the peas on top of it.

❽ Chop the ham into ¼-inch (6 mm) squares, and place in one of the silicone baking cups. Fill the second cup with Cheerios and place both cups in the second tier of the bento box.

FROZEN PEAS AND CORN

Frozen peas and corn are both convenient items to keep on hand for use in a bento box. Though these vegetables are usually eaten warm, many children enjoy—or at least, don't mind— eating them cold in a bento box. You can run the vegetables under warm water for a minute or two to thaw them out in the morning, or pack them into a bento box while they're still frozen. They will thaw by lunchtime and will help keep the rest of the lunch at a safe temperature until it is time to eat.

Woodland Bento Box

Mr. Hedgehog and Mr. Squirrel are visiting with each other in the Great Bento Forest. They're enjoying the scenery – broccoli trees, radish mushrooms, edamame pebbles, and some pretty cheese flowers!

INGREDIENTS

Sliced whole-wheat bread
Desired sandwich fillings
Sliced white bread
Mayonnaise
Raw or lightly steamed
    broccoli
Cooked and shelled edamame
Sugar snap peas
2 radishes
Dried cranberries
Sliced cheddar cheese

EQUIPMENT

Single-tier bento box
Medium hedgehog cutter
Small circle cutter
Black food-safe marker
Small squirrel cutter
Extra-small flower cutter
Extra-small circle cutter

❶ Cut two hedgehog shapes from the bread. Make a hedgehog-shaped sandwich using your desired fillings.

❷ Using a drinking glass or a rolling pin flatten a piece of white bread and then cut out a hedgehog shape. Use the small circle cutter to cut off the face of the white bread hedgehog. Discard the rest of the white bread. Use the black food-safe marker to draw an eye, nose, and mouth on the face piece. Dab mayonnaise on the back of the face piece and place it on top of the sandwich. Place the hedgehog sandwich in the middle of the box.

❸ Tuck in a piece of broccoli on either side of the sandwich.

❹ Place a layer of edamame underneath the hedgehog.

❺ Cut the sugar snap peas in half lengthwise and place them vertically around the broccoli stems.

❻ Place radish mushrooms (see this page) on the edamame.

❼ Fill the empty space above the hedgehog with dried cranberries.

❽ Cut a small squirrel and three flowers from the cheese. Put the squirrel on one of the broccoli trees and the flowers on top of the edamame.

HOW TO MAKE A RADISH MUSHROOM

1. Trim the root and stem ends from a radish.

2. Insert a ½-inch (1.25 cm) round cookie cutter into the stem end of the radish.

3. Leaving the cutter in place and pointing straight up, slide the knife into the radish parallel to the cutting board. Insert the knife just until it hits the cutter. Leaving the cutter in the radish will keep the stem round and will keep you from accidentally cutting all the way through the radish. Rotate the radish to cut it all the way around.

4. Pull the cut piece of radish up to make sure it's cut all the way around, then slowly and gently remove the cutter.

5. The radish will look like a mushroom now! You can use it as is, or decorate it.

6. To make stripes, cut a slim trough from the top of the radish down to the edge. Continue cutting stripes all the way around the top of the radish.

BENTOS
FOR ALL
SEASONS

Lovey-Dovey Lunch

Valentine's Day calls for a little extra sweetness at lunchtime! A colorful bento box filled with hearts will let your child know that lunch was packed with lots of love.

INGREDIENTS
Popcorn
Valentine-themed sprinkles
Small pink or red candies
Apple
Red fruit leather
Strawberries
Sliced whole-wheat bread
Desired sandwich fillings

EQUIPMENT
Single-tier bento box with
    inner containers
Small wedge-shaped
    silicone cup
Small heart cutter
Large heart cutter

❶ Fill one of the larger inner containers of the bento box with the popcorn. Decorate the popcorn evenly with the sprinkles.

❷ Fill the small silicone cup with the candies and place in one of the smaller inner containers. Cut a chunk of apple to fit inside the container with the candies.

❸ Score the skin of the apple chunk with the small heart cutter. Remove the cutter, then slide the tip of the paring knife under the part of the skin you've just cut. Carefully cut through the apple underneath the heart shape by rotating the apple and keeping your knife in the groove you created with the cutter just underneath the apple skin. When you've gone all the way around the shape, pop the heart-shaped piece of skin out and discard.

❹ Using the same small cutter, cut a heart shape from the fruit leather. Place the cutout in the space you've cut into the apple.

❺ Cut small slices from the rest of the apple. Use them to fill the space in the container with the candies. Place the chunk of apple decorated with the heart on top.

❻ Cut a V-shape into the top of the strawberries to hull them. Cut the strawberries in half from top to bottom to approximate a heart shape. Place these in a single layer inside the second small inner container.

❼ If you'd like to add a few perfectly heart-shaped strawberries to the top of the strawberry container, lay a hulled and halved strawberry flat on the cutting board, then cut it with the small heart cutter. This works better with larger strawberries.

❽ Make heart-shaped sandwiches by cutting the bread with the large heart cutter then filling with your desired ingredients. Place the sandwiches in the last empty container.

Bunny Bento

This box of fluffy bunnies celebrates the dawn of spring after the long winter months.

INGREDIENTS
Cooked rice
Small sheet nori seaweed
Peas
Hard-boiled egg
Carrot sticks
Chick-shaped crackers

EQUIPMENT
Two-tier bento box
Rabbit-shaped silicone mold
Nori face punch
Bunny-shaped egg mold
Round silicone baking cup

❶ Pack the cooked rice tightly into the rabbit-shaped silicone mold, pressing down as hard as you can with the back of a spoon. This is easiest to do when the rice has been prepared to be a little bit sticky and is still warm, but you can also use cold rice. Smooth the exposed side of the rice as well as you can. Cover the mold with plastic wrap and refrigerate until completely cooled, or overnight if possible.

❷ When you are ready to pack the lunch, pop a few of the rice bunnies out of the mold.

❸ Trim any brittle or thin edges from the nori using kitchen shears. Punch a face out of the nori and arrange it on the cutting board the way you'd like it to look on your bunny.

❹ Quickly dip the flat side of the rice ball in a small bowl of water. Shake off any excess water and then press the wet side of the rice onto the nori pieces. The face should stick to the rice. Repeat this process to make two more rice bunnies.

❺ Place the bunnies in one tier of the box. Fill in the empty spaces with the peas.

❻ Place a hard-boiled egg that has been molded into a bunny shape (see facing page) in the center of the second tier. Place the carrot sticks on one side of the egg. Fill a silicone cup with the chick-shaped crackers and place on the other side of the egg.

HOW TO SHAPE A HARD-BOILED EGG WITH AN EGG MOLD

1. Begin with an egg mold and a peeled hard-boiled egg. It's best to use an egg that is peeled cleanly and still warm. Cold eggs can be successfully molded too but they take a little while longer to form a distinct shape.

2. Stand the egg on its end in the bottom half of the mold. It's tempting to lay the egg on its side to match the shape of the mold, but the egg will mold better if you close the mold while the egg is upright.

3. Close the egg mold over the top of the upright egg and fasten the mold with its clasp.

4. Put the egg in the refrigerator for a few hours. If you are in a hurry, you can just put the egg mold in a bowl of iced water for 10–15 minutes.

5. Open the egg mold. Some of the white may have squished out beyond the mold shape—if so, just scrape the extra bits off with a knife.

Flower Bouquet Bento Box

A colorful bouquet made of fruit and cheese greets you when you open this bento box. While the sandwiches look complicated, they are easy to assemble with a few flower-shaped cutters and a couple of slices of cheese.

INGREDIENTS
Clementine or mandarin orange wedges
Blueberries
Sugar snap peas
Yellow bell pepper strips
Sliced whole-wheat bread
Desired sandwich fillings and condiments
Sliced cheddar cheese
Sliced muenster or other white cheese

EQUIPMENT
Two-tier bento box
Round silicone baking cup
Flower cutters in various sizes

❶ Set five clementine wedges to one side and put the rest of the wedges in the silicone cup.

❷ Arrange the remaining five clementine wedges in an overlapping circle around the edge of the cup.

❸ Add a few blueberries to the center of the clementine cup to make a flower. Place the cup at the end of one tier of the box.

❹ Place a few sugar snap peas crosswise across the bottom of the same tier to represent grass. Place one sugar snap pea vertically between the clementine flower and the "grass" to represent a flower stem. Fill in the remaining space in the box with the yellow bell pepper strips.

❺ For the sandwich, cut four flowers from the bread with the largest flower cutter. These pieces should be slightly smaller than the width of the second tier of the bento box.

❻ Assemble two flower-shaped sandwiches with your desired fillings and condiments, taking care to align the top and bottom pieces of bread so they match up.

❼ Cut three or four flowers of different sizes from both the orange and the white cheese, tucking any leftover scraps of cheese inside the sandwiches if you like.

❽ Layer the flower-shaped pieces of cheese on top of the sandwiches alternating colors and choosing a smaller flower for each layer. Place the sandwiches at each end of the second tier of the box.

❾ Fill in the space between the sandwiches with the remaining blueberries.

First Day of School Bento

Surprise your child with a school-themed lunch on his first day back in class. A back to school message, a cheerful bus, and a reminder to study spelled out in crackers will all make him happier to be back at a desk and starting a new year of learning.

INGREDIENTS
Sliced whole-wheat bread
Desired sandwich fillings
Sliced white cheese such as Havarti, provolone, or muenster
Sliced cheddar cheese
Cucumber
Nectarine
Cheese crackers with letters

EQUIPMENT
Single-tier divided bento box with a round inner container
Small alphabet cutters
Bus stamping-cutter
Alphabet decorative picks

Variation If a cheese decoration isn't a good match for your sandwich fillings (for example a peanut butter and jelly sandwich) cut the decorative letters out of fruit leather and glue them to the bread with honey.

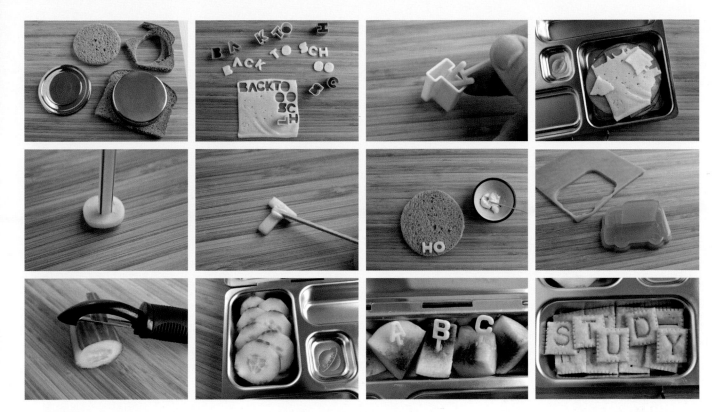

❶ Use the round container from the largest section in the bento box to cut two circle shapes from the bread. Using the container that came with the box ensures that the sandwich will fit perfectly into that section of the box.

❷ Assemble the sandwich using your desired fillings.

❸ Cut the letters to spell out "back to school" from the white cheese. If you like, you can remove the center from the *O*'s using the end of a drinking straw. Use the dull end of a decorative pick to gently poke out the cheese if it gets stuck. You can tuck any leftover scraps of cheese into the sandwich.

❹ Spell out "back to school" along the outside edge of the top slice of bread. Begin by choosing the two middle letters in the bottom word (in this case the *H* and the first *O*) and position them in the middle of the bread. Add letters from the center out to the ends, spreading a small dab of mayonnaise on the back of each letter to glue it to the bread. Repeat this process using the rest of the letters to spell out the remaining words across the top of the bread.

❺ Cut a bus shape from the cheddar cheese using the outer part of the bus cutter. Center the stamping piece of the cutter over the bus shape and press it into the cheese to imprint the bus details. Place the bus in the middle of the bread. Put the sandwich in the largest section of the box.

❻ Peel the cucumber leaving on a few thin strips of skin. Slice into rounds. Place the slices in the upper left section of the box, arranging them so that the green skin makes an attractive pattern.

❼ Cut the nectarines into chunks and put them in the upper right section of the bento box, decorating with alphabet picks.

❽ Fill the remaining section of the box with the cheese crackers. Arrange a few crackers on the top of the pile to spell out the word "study."

Autumn Leaf Bento

The air is crisp, the leaves are changing, and squirrels are scurrying around preparing for winter! Send your little one to school with this autumn-themed bento box to celebrate the season.

INGREDIENTS
Sliced whole-wheat bread
Sliced cheddar cheese
Apple
Mango chutney
Red, orange, and yellow bell
    pepper pieces
Hummus

EQUIPMENT
Single-tier bento box
Medium squirrel cutter
Small acorn cutter
Two small side-dish
    containers
Small leaf cutters
Scarecrow decorative pick

❶ Use squirrel cutter to cut four squirrel shapes from the bread.

❷ Cut two squirrel shapes and an acorn shape from the cheese.

❸ Cut four large, thin slices of apple by slicing the apple vertically, close to the core. Cut squirrel shapes from the slices. You may need to cut a top half and a bottom half of the squirrel and overlap them to get a full squirrel shape.

❹ Spread two slices of the squirrel-shaped bread with chutney. Top with cheese squirrels, cheese scraps, and apple slices, and the last two pieces of squirrel bread.

❺ Place the sandwiches at the far side of the bento box so that they face each other. Put the acorn-shaped cheese on top of the sandwiches.

❻ Peel the bell pepper and cut out leaf shapes. Put chopped pepper scraps at the bottom of the near side of the bento box. Put the leaves on top of the scraps. Reserve one leaf.

❼ Fill one of the small side-dish containers with the desired amount of hummus. Top with the reserved pepper leaf.

❽ Chop the remainder of the apple into chunks and treat with one of the anti-browning techniques on page 65. Dry well and place in the second of the small side-dish containers. Spear a few apple pieces onto the scarecrow pick and place on top.

Variation *Substitute any favorite dip for the hummus.*

Tip *The skin on bell peppers is tough and can be difficult to cut with cutters. Remove the skin from bell peppers with a vegetable peeler before cutting into shapes to ensure clean edges.*

Halloween Bento Box

A jack-o'-lantern sandwich, a pile of pumpkins, a witch, and her green "potion" all come together to make this spooky Halloween meal. Be sure to start preparing this bento no later than the night before you are planning to eat it so that the gelatin will have time to set in the refrigerator.

INGREDIENTS
Green gelatin
Small black grapes
Cantaloupe
Sliced whole-wheat bread
Sliced turkey or other deli meat
Desired sandwich condiments
Sliced cheddar cheese
Raisins

EQUIPMENT
Single-tier bento box with three sections
Small pumpkin cutter
Witch decorative pick
Large pumpkin cutter
Jack-o'-lantern eye and mouth cutters
Plastic spider ring

Variations *If you don't have black grapes on hand, grapes of another color or blueberries will look just as creepy in the gelatin.*

❶ Prepare the gelatin according to the package directions. Fill the smallest section of the bento box half-full of gelatin. Add the grapes to the gelatin, cover the box, and place in the refrigerator for at least four hours or until the gelatin is fully set.

❷ Cut the cantaloupe into ¼-inch (6 mm) thick slices. Cut several pumpkin shapes from the slices using the small cutter. Chop the remaining cantaloupe, discarding the rind, and place in the bottom of the other small section of the bento box. Place the pumpkin-shaped pieces of cantaloupe on top and spear one of them with a witch pick.

❸ Cut two pumpkin shapes from the bread using the large cutter. Use the jack-o'-lantern eye and mouth cutters to make a pumpkin face in one of the pumpkin-shaped pieces of bread.

❹ Layer the deli meat and any desired condiments on top of the pumpkin shape without a face. Center a slice of cheddar cheese on top. Cut off any meat or cheese that overhangs the edge of the bread and slip the scraps under the slice of cheese. Put the bread with the pumpkin face on top and place in the large section of the bento box.

❺ Fill in the spaces around the sandwich with raisins. Add the spider ring for decoration.

Snowman Bento Box

Friendly snowmen smile up from this wintry bento box especially for vegetarians.

INGREDIENTS
Teriyaki baked tofu
Carrot sticks
Naan or other flatbread
Green grapes

EQUIPMENT
Two-tier bento box with divider
Small circle cutter
Small house cutter
Black and orange food-safe markers
Snowman decorative pick

Variation If you prefer not to use tofu to make the main snowman, you can achieve a similar effect by assembling a sandwich using one piece of white bread for the snowman and one piece of whole-wheat bread for the border around it.

BAKED TOFU
If tofu is not a food your family eats, teriyaki baked tofu is an excellent introduction to this ingredient. This ready-made tofu has been marinated in teriyaki sauce before baking, giving it a sweet, nutty flavor and a firm, meaty texture. It's delicious eaten plain, as in this bento box, but you can also mix it into soups, stir-fries, or salads. Find it in the Asian or health food section of the grocery store.

❶ Slice a layer about ⅛-inch (3 mm) thick off the broad side of the block of tofu. Cut a small circle from the center of the tofu slice and set aside. Place the circle cutter close to the bottom edge of the tofu slice, overlapping the hole you just cut. Cut a crescent shape from the tofu and set aside. Place the house cutter with the pointed side down near the top of the tofu slice. Cut out a hat shape and set aside.

❷ Draw eyes and a mouth on the white side of the circle-shaped tofu using the black food-safe marker. Draw a carrot nose with the orange marker.

❸ Add two or three buttons to the crescent of tofu using the black marker.

❹ Color the white side of the hat piece of tofu black with the marker. If you have trouble keeping the ink flowing from the marker, dab it gently on a paper towel to remove any excess moisture that has accumulated on it."

❺ Flip the piece of tofu that the snowman pieces were cut from so that the brown side is up. Carefully place the snowman pieces into their empty spaces. Slice the thicker piece of tofu into strips and carefully place the snowman and its border on top of the block of sliced tofu. Place in the center of

one of the tiers of the bento box.

❻ Place carrot sticks in the box on either side of the snowman.

❼ Using the same small circle cutter, cut the flatbread into rounds. Separate the second tier of the bento box into two with the divider and arrange several plain rounds of flatbread on one side. Using the food-safe markers, draw snowman faces on several more circles of bread. Place the decorated bread on top of the plain bread.

❽ Fill the remaining space in the bento box with grapes. Arrange a few grapes on a decorative snowman pick and place on top.

Gingerbread Man Bento

This happy gingerbread man lunch is a fun way to kick off the holiday season. Though it conjures up the idea of sweets and Christmas festivities, it's filled with healthy foods anyone would enjoy.

INGREDIENTS
Sliced pumpernickel bread
Sliced Swiss cheese
Sliced pastrami
Mayonnaise
Yogurt pretzels
Sugar snap peas
Grape tomatoes

EQUIPMENT
Single-tier bento box
Gingerbread man cutter
Extra-small circle cutter or drinking straw
Extra-small bow-tie cutter
Silicone food divider
Gingerbread man decorative pick

Variation *Substitute a gingerbread man for a gingerbread woman and have fun adding hair or decorating her dress. This is something kids love to help with.*

BENTOS FOR ALL SEASONS

❶ Cut two gingerbread shapes from the bread, one from the cheese and one from the pastrami. Assemble the sandwich.

❷ Cut four extra-small circles, four small rectangles, a crescent, and a bow tie from the cheese scraps. If you don't have a crescent cutter, use a small circle or the rounded part of a heart cutter to cut a piece from the edge of the cheese (see photo above). Use the same cutter to cut the piece of cheese into a crescent shape.

❸ Arrange the cheese shapes on top of the sandwich as shown in the photo: two circles for eyes, the crescent for the mouth, the bow tie and two circles to decorate the shirt, and the rectangles as decorations on the arms and legs. Glue the cheese in place with mayonnaise and place the sandwich in the box.

❹ Tuck a few yogurt pretzels into the top of the box. Stand the silicone divider up next to the pretzels to separate them from the vegetables.

❺ Pack a few rows of sugar snap peas next to the divider.

❻ Thread a few tomatoes on the gingerbread man pick. Place the pick below the peas and then fill the space around it with more tomatoes.

Christmas Tree Bento

Fill your child's backpack with holiday cheer when you make this festive bento. The tree is assembled using veggies, cheese, and a small piece of pretzel stick, while the faux candy canes and peppermint drops are made from bread, salami, and cheese.

INGREDIENTS
Flatbread
6 large slices salami
Sliced Havarti cheese
Pretzel stick
Sugar snap peas
Red bell pepper piece

EQUIPMENT
Two-tier bento box
Small candy cane cutter
Red food-safe marker
Christmas tree decorative pick
Small star cutter
Extra-small star cutter

Variations *Ornaments for the tree can be cut from other types of vegetables. Thin slices of carrot, cucumber, tomato, or jicama would all work well.*

❶ Cut four candy-cane shapes from a piece of flatbread. Use the red food-safe marker to draw stripes on the bread. Place some scraps of the bread at one end of one tier of the box. Cut another piece of bread to fit in the box over the scraps. Top with the decorated pieces of bread.

❷ Fold a slice of salami in half, and then cut a piece of cheese to fit on top of it. Roll up the salami and cheese into a tight bundle. Repeat to make five more roll-ups. Stand the roll-ups on end in the empty space below the bread, spearing one of them with the Christmas tree decorative pick.

❸ Place a small piece of pretzel stick at the near end of the second tier of the bento box. This will represent the trunk of the Christmas tree. Arrange the sugar snap peas above the pretzel to mimic the leaves of a fir tree.

❹ Cut a small star from a scrap of cheese and place it at the top tip of the tree. Peel the red bell pepper, cut a thin slice, and punch stars from it using the extra-small star cutter. Arrange the star "ornaments" on the tree.

Christmas Gift Bento Box

Ho ho ho! Santa Claus is coming to lunch and he's bringing lots of gifts! Christmas-crazy kids will appreciate opening this box to find red and green fruit and a stack of cheese-and-cracker packages.

INGREDIENTS

Kiwi

Pomegranate seeds

Cubed ham

Sliced Havarti cheese

Red bell pepper, roasted and peeled

Crackers

EQUIPMENT

Single-tier bento box

Round silicone baking cup

Santa decorative pick

Reindeer decorative pick

❶ Peel the kiwi, cut into bite-sized chunks, and toss with the pomegranate seeds. Place the fruit in the silicone cup and put the cup in the upper left corner of the bento box.

❷ Fill the space in the lower left corner of the bento box with the ham. Thread a few cubes of ham onto the Santa and reindeer picks and arrange them on top of the pile.

❸ Cut the cheese into squares that are slightly smaller than the crackers. Cut four very thin strips of roasted red bell

pepper. Drain the bell pepper strips on a piece of paper towel to remove any excess moisture.

❹ Lay the bell pepper strips on two of the cheese squares, crossing them in the middle so they resemble ribbons on a package. Trim any pepper hanging over the edge of the cheese with a sharp knife, then place these cheese "gifts" on two of the crackers.

❺ Place layers of crackers and cheese in the remaining space in the box. Top with the two decorated crackers.

BENTOS FOR ALL SEASONS

BENTOS FOR GROWN-UPS

Antipasti Bento

This sophisticated lunch will be the envy of the office break room. It's easy to assemble and many of the components can be stored for weeks in jars in the refrigerator so this is a menu that can be thrown together when you're low on perishables. Don't forget to pack a small fork or spoon so you can dish the antipasti onto the bread!

INGREDIENTS

Sliced country-style bread
Olive oil
½ clove garlic, peeled
Cantaloupe
Prosciutto
Assorted small heirloom tomatoes
Ciliegine (small balls of mozzarella)
Marinated artichoke hearts
Mixed olives
Jarred roasted red pepper

EQUIPMENT

Two-tier bento box with divider
3 square silicone baking cups
Fork to eat with

Variations If you don't have all of these items on hand, substitute items you do have in your fridge. Any kind of olive works well, as do leftover roasted veggies. Add a small container of pesto or tapenade to spread on the bread for extra flavor.

❶ Lightly brush the bread with olive oil. Toast in a toaster oven until lightly browned.

❷ Rub the garlic over the oiled side of the bread while still warm. Let the bread cool, and then put into one tier of the bento box.

❸ Cut the cantaloupe into wedges that fit the width of the bento box. Cut a slice of prosciutto lengthwise into 1-inch (2.5 cm) strips. Wrap each slice of cantaloupe with one of the prosciutto strips and place in the bento box next to the bread. Use the divider to keep the bread and the cantaloupe separate.

❹ Slice the tomatoes and the ciliegine into halves. Mix them together and place in one of the silicone cups in the second tier of the bento box.

❺ Drain the marinated artichoke hearts and the olives, arrange in separate silicone cups, and place inside the bento box. Fill the remaining empty spaces with slices of roasted red pepper.

Artful Leftovers

Dinner leftovers are a bento box staple, but they don't have to be boring. For this lunch the bits and pieces of a taco dinner are arranged in an attractive way that gives them new life. To save time in the mornings, pack leftovers right into a bento box as you're cleaning up from the evening meal.

INGREDIENTS
Tortillas
Chopped tomatoes
Shredded lettuce
Leftover taco meat (I used
    chicken here)
Sour cream
Shredded cheese
Hot sauce

EQUIPMENT
Single-tier bento box with divider
2 square silicone baking cups
Small, lidded cup
Sauce bottle
Fork to eat with

❶ Fold the tortillas in half and roll them up. Tuck them into one end of the bento box and hold them in place with the divider.

❷ Put the tomatoes and lettuce in separate silicone cups. Place them at the opposite end of the bento box to the tortillas.

❸ Arrange the chicken in the bento box next to the tomatoes and lettuce.

❹ Fill the small, lidded cup with the sour cream. Place it in the box between the divider and the chicken.

❺ Fill the remaining space with the shredded cheese.

❻ Fill the sauce bottle with hot sauce (see facing page) and nestle it into the pile of cheese.

FILLING A SAUCE BOTTLE

Sauce bottles often have very small openings and it can be difficult to pour liquid into them without spilling it. Here's how to fill these tiny containers with no mess:

1. Fill a small bowl with the liquid you'd like to put in the sauce bottle. The lid of the bottle of liquid works well for this too.
2. Squeeze the wide end of the dropper included with the sauce bottle to remove as much air as possible.
3. Insert the tip of the dropper into the liquid, and then let go of the wide end. The dropper will fill up with sauce.
4. Insert the tip of the dropper into the neck of the sauce bottle and then squeeze the wide end to expel it.
5. Repeat this process until the bottle is filled.

Cheese Plate Bento Box

Pack this easy bento box for a day in the park with friends or for an elegant snack when travelling.

INGREDIENTS
Brie cheese
Aged salami
Clementine
Water crackers
Aged Gouda cheese
Grapes
Roasted almonds

EQUIPMENT
Single-tier bento box
Small spreader or cheese knife to use while eating

Variations This box is ripe for interpretation! Swap out the Brie with a small round of goat cheese or substitute any other hard cheese you like for the Gouda.

❶ Cut a wedge of the Brie, slice off the tip, and place it in the bento box.

❷ Cut slices of the salami until you have a stack the same height as the bento box.

❸ Place the Brie and the salami in two corners of the bento box with a clementine between them. The fruit will act as a natural divider and will help keep the flavors of the meat and the cheese from mingling too much.

❹ Place a stack of crackers above the clementine.

❺ Cut a chunk of the Gouda to fit in the corner between the crackers and the salami. Slice the Gouda chunk and tuck the slices into the box.

❻ Fill the remaining large space with the grapes. Fill any remaining gaps with the almonds.

Family Picnic Bento

Bentos aren't always single serve! Pack a lunch for the whole family in a large picnic-style bento box and bring it along on an outing to the park or zoo. The compact design of the bento box allows you to pack all your al fresco favorites – chicken, fruit salad, and muffins – in a small, easy-to-carry package.

INGREDIENTS

Chicken drumsticks
Barbecue sauce
**2 mandarin oranges, peeled and
    separated into segments**
½ pint (200 g) blueberries
3 kiwis, peeled and chopped
Assorted cookies
Mini corn muffins

EQUIPMENT

Multi-tier stacking bento box
**Forks or spoons for the fruit
    salad**

Tip *Perk up a boxed muffin mix by
stirring in ⅓ cup (50 g) each of
frozen corn and diced red bell
pepper.*

❶ Preheat the broiler to low. Place the chicken on a foil-lined baking sheet. Roast for 20 minutes on each side or until the chicken is cooked through.

❷ Baste one side of the chicken with the barbecue sauce and roast for an additional 2–3 minutes, taking care not to burn the sauce. Turn the chicken over, baste the other side with sauce,

and cook for a further 2–3 minutes. Remove the chicken from the oven and allow to cool completely.

❸ Pack the chicken legs in the largest container of the bento box.

❹ Toss the oranges, blueberries, and kiwi in a large bowl to make a fruit salad. Split the fruit salad between two of the smaller bento box containers.

❺ Pack the cookies into the third small container, alternating lighter and darker cookies.

❻ Place the mini muffins in the remaining small container.

❼ Put the lids on the containers and stack into the outer carrier.

Flower Garden Bento

A snack-y lunch of salami, crackers, vegetables, and dip becomes a work of art when you turn it into a flower garden. Humble salami is transformed into a rose and the bright colors of the veggies lend themselves to a floral treatment.

INGREDIENTS
Sliced salami
Flower-shaped crackers
Red bell pepper
Yellow bell pepper
Carrot
Sugar snap peas
Hummus
Raw or lightly steamed broccoli

EQUIPMENT
Two-tier bento box
2 round silicone baking cups
Small flower cutter
Extra-small circle cutter

Tip It may seem like you're looking for a mess if you put a cup of hummus in your bento box with no lid but if you choose the right sized cup it won't spill. Look for a cup the same height as the outer wall of the bento box. When you put the lid on the bento box, it will fit tightly over both the box and the silicone cup inside and you needn't fear spills.

❶ Assemble the salami rose according to the instructions on this page. Place the salami rose cup in one tier of the box.

❷ Fill the space next to the salami with the crackers.

❸ Cut two large chunks from the bell peppers. Remove their tough skin with a vegetable peeler to make it easier to cut out the shapes. Cut five or six flowers from the two peppers. Peel the carrot and slice into rounds about ¼ inch (6 mm) thick.

❹ Using the circle cutter, remove the center from each of the bell pepper flowers. Using the same cutter, cut circles from the carrot slices.

❺ Add the circular carrot and pepper pieces to the middles of the flowers, taking care to vary the color combinations.

❻ Slice the sugar snap peas diagonally to make leaf shapes.

❼ Fill the second silicone cup with hummus. Arrange one of the pepper flowers and a few of the sugar snap pea "leaves" on top. Place the hummus in the second tier of the box.

❽ Fill the remaining space in the second tier with a layer of broccoli.

❾ Arrange the pepper flowers and a few sugar snap peas on top of the broccoli.

HOW TO MAKE A ROSE FROM SLICED DELI MEAT

These decorative roses look complicated but come together very quickly. They can be made with nearly any kind of sliced deli meat, but the pinkish hues of ham and salami tend to make the prettiest flowers.

1. *Begin with a round silicone cup and six or seven slices of salami. Fold a slice of salami in half and press it against the side of the cup.*

2. *Fold a second slice of salami and place it in the cup, slightly overlapping the first slice.*

3. *Continue working your way around the circle, folding and overlapping until the space in the middle is about a ½ inch (1.25 cm) in diameter.*

4. *Fold the final piece of salami in half, and roll it up tightly into a cone shape. Insert the cone into the middle of the flower and fan it out slightly to fill in the space.*

5. *Use the same technique to make a ham rose, but use two slices of ham cut into a total of eight strips.*

Bagel and Lox Bento

Bring the deli to your desk! Pack a bagel, lox, and a few scoops of cream cheese with some fresh figs and a quick-and-easy Mediterranean salad.

INGREDIENTS
Bagel
Cream cheese
Capers
Lox
Fresh figs
Simple Mediterranean Salad (see below)

EQUIPMENT
Four-tier stacking bento box set
1-tablespoon kitchen scoop
Round silicone baking cup
Small wedge-shaped silicone cup

Variations Vary the toppings to suit your tastes. Consider swapping sliced red onion for the capers or adding a few slices of ripe tomato.

❶ Pack the bagel in one tier of the bento box.

❷ Place two balls of scooped cheese in the round cup. Put in the second tier of the box. Put the capers in the wedge-shaped cup and place in the same tier. Fill the rest of the space with lox.

❸ Cut the figs into wedges and place in the third tier.

❹ Fill the final tier of the box with Simple Mediterranean Salad (see below). Don't forget to pack a knife and fork!

Simple Mediterranean Salad

INGREDIENTS
½ cup (75 g) halved cherry tomatoes
½ cup (60 g) diced cucumber
2 teaspoons vinaigrette
2 tablespoons feta cheese

Toss the tomatoes and cucumber with the vinaigrette. Sprinkle with the feta cheese.

Pinwheels

Bring sunshine to a dreary day with this colorful lunch packed with a rainbow of fruits and vegetables.

INGREDIENTS
8-inch (20 cm) whole-wheat tortilla
3 tablespoons Curried Cream Cheese
Thinly sliced turkey
¼ avocado, sliced lengthwise
Yellow bell pepper strips
Grated carrot
Sliced tomato
Grapes
Crackers
Orange slices

EQUIPMENT
Single-tier bento box
Round silicone baking cup

Variations *If you don't have all of the vegetables listed here on hand, substitute whatever you happen to have in your crisper. Spinach, cucumber spears, finely chopped broccoli, or sugar snap peas would all work wonderfully in this bento.*

❶ Lightly toast the tortilla in a skillet on the stove or in a toaster oven. Cook it just long enough to take off the floury taste, but not so long that it crisps up and is no longer pliable.

❷ Cool the tortilla and spread evenly with Curried Cream Cheese (see below).

❸ Lay the sliced turkey on one half of the tortilla, then add the avocado, pepper, carrot, and tomato in vertical strips across the tortilla starting at the turkey side and stopping about 1 inch (2.5 cm) from the opposite edge. This last area should be bare of turkey and vegetables so the cream cheese can glue the tortilla shut.

❹ Fold the edge of the tortilla over the avocado slices, and then continue to roll it tightly to form a tube. You may need to tuck the vegetables in as you roll to keep them in place.

❺ Cut the tube crosswise into eight 1-inch (2.5 cm) slices.

❻ Pack four of the slices next to each other along the far edge of the bento box. (Use the other four spirals in a second lunch or reserve them to use in tomorrow's lunch.)

❼ Put the grapes into the silicone cup and pack it into the box along with a stack of crackers and the orange slices.

Curried Cream Cheese

INGREDIENTS
4 oz (100 g) ⅓ less fat cream cheese
1 tablespoon milk
¼ teaspoon garlic powder
1 teaspoon curry powder

Combine all the ingredients in a food processor. Pulse to combine, scraping down the sides of the processor frequently.

Pretty Salad Bento Box

Salads are a lunch-box staple but there's no reason they have to be routine. Add a bit of whimsy to your daily greens by sprinkling them with pretty carrot flowers. Additional toppings of salmon and avocado add protein and healthy fats to leave you feeling satisfied at the end of your meal.

INGREDIENTS
Mixed salad greens
Grape tomatoes
Large carrot
½ avocado
Smoked salmon
Salad dressing
Olive bread

EQUIPMENT
Single-tier bento box with inner containers
Small metal flower cutter
Small, lidded sauce cup
Knife and fork to eat with

Variations Many vegetables hold up well when sliced and cut into pretty shapes. Try cutting peppers or cucumbers as well as carrots.

❶ Place the salad greens in the largest container of the bento box. Cut the grape tomatoes in half and arrange on top of the lettuce.

❷ Peel the carrot and slice into thin rounds. Cut flower shapes using the cutter. Arrange the carrot flowers on top of the salad.

❸ Fill the avocado cavity with the smoked salmon. Place in one of the smaller containers of the bento box.

❹ Fill the small, lidded sauce cup with the salad dressing and tuck into the remaining empty container of the bento box along with a few slices of the olive bread.

Sausage and Salad Bento

A bento box with removable inner containers opens up many options for packed lunches. Pull out individual containers and pop them in the microwave if you'd like to eat the contents warm, or remove a few to accommodate larger items such as salads.

INGREDIENTS
Mini-baguette
One large, fully cooked sausage
Salad dressing
Arugula
Pecans
Dried cranberries
Goat cheese

EQUIPMENT
Single-tier bento box with inner
** containers**
Small, lidded sauce cup
Medium star cutter
Small piece of waxed paper or
** parchment**
Knife and fork to eat with

Variations If time is tight while you're packing this lunch, you can simply slice the goat cheese into a circle or crumble it over the salad rather than shaping it into a star.

❶ Cut the baguette into lengths that will fit into one of the inner containers. Arrange the baguette pieces in the container and place inside the bento box.

❷ Cut the sausage in half crosswise, and then cut each half into two pieces lengthwise. Slice the quartered sausage into smaller chunks.

❸ Layer half of the sausage chunks on the bottom of a second inner container, as evenly as possible. Arrange the remaining sausage chunks in two rows on top of the base layer, turning every other row skin side up to form a pattern of light and dark stripes. Place this container next to the container holding the baguette.

❹ Fill the small, lidded sauce cup with the salad dressing and tuck it in a corner of the largest bento box container. Fill the remaining space with arugula, sprinkling the pecans and cranberries on top.

❺ Place the star cutter on the waxed paper. Pack the goat cheese into the cutter with a spoon and level off the top.

❻ Lift the cutter while gently pressing on the top of the cheese with your fingertips to ease it out. If a corner sticks, press down with the handle of the spoon to loosen it. Once the cheese is out of the cutter, reshape it with your fingers if necessary, then nestle the cheese into the top of the salad.

Savory Bread Pudding Bento

Use leftovers and scraps to create the delicious and economical Savory Bread Pudding featured in this lunch. It's a dish that tastes great heated if you have access to a microwave at lunchtime, but it's just as enjoyable served cold. Round out the meal with some fruit, pretty carrot strips, and a few cookies.

INGREDIENTS
Savory Bread Pudding (see facing page)
Carrot
Grapes
Cookies
Strawberry
Sliced muenster cheese

EQUIPMENT
Single-tier bento box
Vegetable peeler
Two square silicone baking cups
Small heart cutter
Fork to eat with

❶ Cut a piece of Savory Bread Pudding (see facing page) to fill about half the bento box and place it inside.

❷ Peel the carrot and use a vegetable peeler to cut the carrot into long, thin strips. Fold and twist the carrot strips into accordion and spiral shapes and arrange them in one of the silicone cups. Place the cup in the bento box next to the Savory Bread Pudding.

❸ Fill the second cup with the grapes and place it next to the carrots.

❹ Fill remaining space in the box with the cookies and the strawberry.

❺ Cut a heart shape from the cheese and place it on top of the pudding.

Savory Bread Pudding

This recipe is extremely flexible so it's a good way to use up any scraps you have saved from assembling decorative lunches – particularly extra pieces of bread that are left over when you cut a sandwich with a cutter. I save my bread scraps in a resealable bag in the freezer until I have enough to make this dish. You can use just about any combination of vegetables too, so it's a good way to put bits and pieces from the crisper to use as well.

INGREDIENTS

3 cups (90 g)dried bread cubes

3 eggs, beaten

¾ cup (180 ml) milk

½ teaspoon salt

½ teaspoon thyme

1½ cups (200 g) assorted diced vegetables, such as broccoli, tomato, bell pepper, zucchini, spinach, or cooked winter squash

3 oz (85 g) diced ham or sausage (optional)

3 oz (85 g) finely chopped or grated cheese, such as cheddar, muenster, Swiss, Gouda, or Havarti

❶ If the bread is still soft and pliable, begin by drying it in the oven. Spread the bread cubes on a cookie sheet and place in the oven for 40–45 minutes at 225°F (110°C) until crisp.

❷ Heat the oven to 375°F (190°C) degrees. Butter a 9 x 9–inch (22 x 22 cm) baking dish.

❸ In a large bowl, combine the eggs, milk, salt, and thyme. Add the vegetables, the meat (if using), and 2 oz (55 g) of the cheese. Mix well.

❹ Add the bread cubes to the mixture and toss gently to combine. Let the mixture sit for 10 minutes, stirring occasionally, to give the bread a chance to absorb some of the egg mixture.

❺ Transfer the mixture to the greased baking dish and sprinkle with the remaining cheese.

❻ Bake for 40–45 minutes or until the egg mixture is set and the cheese is bubbly.

Tiny Sandwiches

Tiny sandwiches are a great way to use up small amounts of leftovers at the end of the week. A couple of slices of salami, a bit of cheese, a dab of mustard, or the last few veggies in the crisper can all be combined in innovative ways to make a delicious and thrifty lunch.

INGREDIENTS

Sugar snap peas
8 thin slices baguette
Assorted sandwich fillings—I used
  egg salad, turkey and cheddar,
  ham and Swiss, and cream
  cheese with tomato
Mango

EQUIPMENT

Single-tier bento box
Flower decorative pick
Flower-shaped silicone food
  dividers

Variations I used thinly sliced baguette for the bread here, but cocktail bread would work well too. If the breadbox is empty, you could use crackers instead.

❶ Place a single layer of sugar snap peas across three-quarters of the bottom of the bento box.

❷ Lay out four slices of baguette and top with various fillings. You can make them all different, all the same, or mix and match them however you like. Top with the remaining pieces of bread. Place the sandwiches on top of the peas.

❸ Peel the mango, slice into strips (see facing page), and place it in the empty section of the box. Spear one of the pieces of mango with a flower pick, then insert the silicone flower dividers between the sandwiches and the fruit.

HOW TO CUT A MANGO

Hold the mango upright with the stem end on top. Slice the side of the mango from top to bottom. Turn the mango and cut again on the other side. Trim as much of the remaining fruit off the pit as possible. Cut one of the large chunks of mango in half lengthwise. Remove the flesh by running the knife parallel to the cutting board just above the mango's skin. Repeat with the rest of the fruit. Serve sliced or cubed.

Stripy Bento

This is another bento box that can be put together with common kitchen supplies. A few slices with a knife make an apple more interesting, using two different kinds of bread jazzes up a sandwich, and stacking the vegetables makes for a striking display.

INGREDIENTS
Red apple
Sliced white bread
Sliced whole-wheat bread
Desired sandwich fillings
Cherry tomatoes
Cooked green beans
Jicama sticks
Carrot sticks
Ranch dressing, hummus, or bean dip

EQUIPMENT
Two-tier bento box with divider
Small, lidded container

❶ Cut two chunks of the apple. Cut each chunk into ¼-inch (6 mm) slices. If desired, use one of the anti-browning techniques on page 65 to keep the apple looking fresh. Tuck the slices into the box using the divider, turning over every other slice for a striped effect.

❷ Make your sandwich using one slice of white bread, one slice of whole-wheat bread, and your desired filling. Trim the crusts to make a rectangle. Slice the sandwich into strips. Place the strips in the bento box, turning over alternate slices and staggering them. Fill in the gaps with cherry tomatoes.

❸ Trim the green beans so that they are slightly shorter than the width of the bento box. An easy way to do this is to pile the beans up, place the bento box on top of them, and then trim the beans using the side of the box as a guide. Arrange the green beans at each end of the second tier of the box.

❹ Trim the jicama sticks to the width of the box and arrange them in two piles adjacent to the beans.

❺ Fill the space in the middle of the second tier with carrot sticks. Pour the dip into the small, lidded container and tuck into the remaining space.

Templates

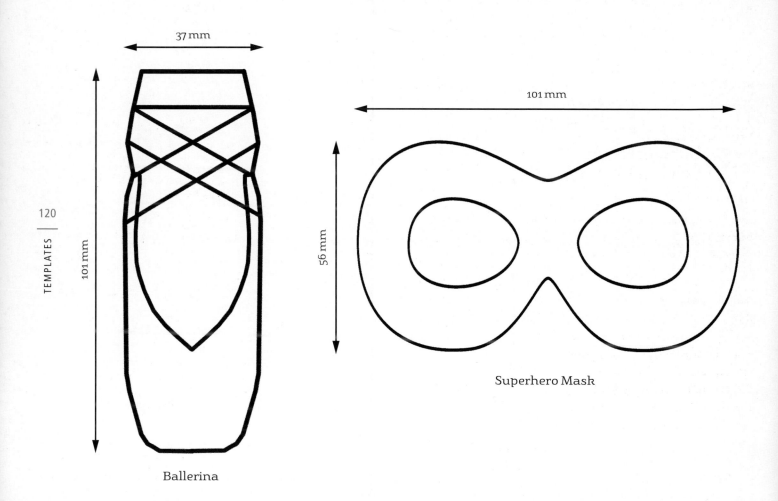

37 mm

101 mm

Ballerina

101 mm

56 mm

Superhero Mask